The Ethical Kaleidoscope

T0293348

The study of corporate governance is a relatively modern development, with significant attention devoted to the subject only during the last fifty years. However, in recent years, awareness of issues and/or shortcomings in the governance of public and private, large and small, for-profit and not-for-profit organisations has become more widespread and, very often, almost instantaneous through social media. This has placed, and is placing, increasing pressure on company directors as they seek to guide their organisations through competitive maelstroms.

Based on research interviews with company chairs in Australia, New Zealand, and the USA, this book considers the challenges faced by directors as they grapple with sometimes competing demands, such as morals and law, personal and corporate values, and the like, in the quest to ensure a successful operation.

The book starts by considering the macro issues of values, ethics, culture, and leadership before moving to consider the microcosm of what actually happens in organisations and the challenges faced by directors. Throughout, the authors provide examples gleaned from their research.

The book concludes by presenting the concept of an ethics kaleidoscope which provides different lenses through which directors can consider issues with which they are faced as they strive to ensure both legality and morality in operations. It then closes with recommendations and tools designed to assist directors as they move forward.

The Ethical Kaleidoscope will be of interest to corporate directors, executives, and shareholders, as well as students of corporate governance and ethics. In other words, it will be of interest to all those who are interested in leading a sustainable culture based on ethics in their organisations.

Douglas G. Long teaches values, ethics, and leadership at the Australian School of Business, University of New South Wales, Sydney, Australia. From 1988 to 2000 he was associated with Macquarie Graduate School of Management in Sydney, where he researched, designed, and delivered the programme Leadership in Senior Management. Two of his previous books, *Delivering High Performance: The Third Generation Organisation* and *Third Generation Leadership and the Locus of Control: Knowledge, Change, and Neuroscience*, were published by Gower. His PhD is in Organisational Psychology.

Zivit Inbar is an Adjunct Professor at the Faculty of Business and Law at Deakin University in Victoria, Australia. She is the owner of DifferenThinking, a boutique consulting service specialising in People and Performance strategies for growth. In addition, Zivit is a Non-Executive Director and Advisory Board Member. Previously, she had an extensive career as Chief Human Resources Officer of global companies. Her PhD is focused on the influence of culture and institutional environment on strategic thinking and strategy in China.

The Ethical Kaleidoscope

Values, Ethics, and Corporate Governance

**Douglas G. Long
and Zivit Inbar**

Routledge
Taylor & Francis Group

LONDON AND NEW YORK

First published 2017
by Routledge
2 Park Square, Milton Park, Abingdon, Oxon OX14 4RN

and by Routledge
711 Third Avenue, New York, NY 10017

First issued in paperback 2018

Routledge is an imprint of the Taylor & Francis Group, an informa business

© 2017 Douglas G. Long and Zivit Inbar

The right of Douglas G. Long and Zivit Inbar to be identified as authors of this work has been asserted by them in accordance with sections 77 and 78 of the Copyright, Designs and Patents Act 1988.

British Library Cataloguing in Publication Data
A catalogue record for this book is available from the British Library

Library of Congress Cataloging in Publication Data
Names: Long, Douglas G., author. | Inbar, Zivit, author.
Title: The ethical kaleidoscope : the role of boards in leading corporate ethics / Douglas Long and Zivit Inbar.
Description: Abingdon, Oxon ; New York, NY : Routledge, 2017.
Identifiers: LCCN 2016028529 | ISBN 9781472471604 (hardback) | ISBN 9781315308838 (ebook)
Subjects: LCSH: Corporate governance—Australia. | Boards of directors—Australia. | Corporations—Moral and ethical aspects—Australia. | Business ethics—Australia.
Classification: LCC HD2741 .L58 2017 | DDC 174/.4—dc23
LC record available at https://lccn.loc.gov/2016028529

ISBN 13: 978-1-138-32016-1 (pbk)
ISBN 13: 978-1-4724-7160-4 (hbk)

Typeset in Bembo
by Book Now Ltd, London

Contents

Introduction

In 2013, at the close of a course on Ethics and Competitive Advantage at the Australian School of Business, University of New South Wales, an international student from a major western European country, came up to Doug and remarked: 'Thank you, Doug, for this course. Until I came here and did this, I never realised that it was possible to be ethical *and* a successful business person.'

A couple of years ago, Zivit published a short blog called 'When change management = change the management'. The idea was that it is all about trust. Trust that the current management can lead the organisation forward and personal trust in the CEO and the executive team. While she received some very positive responses to the blog, those that opposed the idea based their argument on the same notion that boards do not deal in trust. The board's role is strategy, finance, compliance and appointing and managing the CEO.

We would like to argue that these important board roles are based not only on trust, but also on ethics. How do directors know that the financial and other information they receive from the executive team is correct? How do/can they create and govern an ethical organisation? How can they govern organisations that operate in countries that are based on different ethical systems?

Today, society is going through dramatic changes – globalisation, technological advances, social media, social and environmental awareness, investors' involvement – to mention just a few. At the same time, the governance structure within which organisations operate is not changing at the same pace and is both very slow to change and generally reactive rather than proactive. The complexity of governing organisations using an outdated governance structure in a rapidly changing world puts boards at constant risk and facing continual dilemmas, including ethical ones. This book looks at how boards can proactively manage these risks and, by doing so, achieve a strategic advantage.

The book follows on from two of Doug's earlier works:

- First, *Third Generation Leadership and The Locus of Control: Knowledge, Change, and Neuroscience*,[1] which explored the issue of moving our core approach to life from the 'red zone' of reactivity, apprehension and resistance into the 'blue zone' of creativity, innovation and courage – a move which takes us away from an approach to leadership that is dominated by our amygdala to an approach to leadership that is dominated by our prefrontal cortex.
- Second, *Delivering High Performance: The Third Generation Organisation*,[2] which explored the application of third generation leadership to the end of developing and maintaining high performance – both of an organisation itself and, as the means of achieving this, of the people who comprise the organisation. This book (p. 32) also introduced the concept of different leadership responsibilities at differing levels within an organisation. The book makes it clear that the responsibilities of a board are significantly different from those of the executive or management teams and that it is the board, usually epitomised by the chairperson, that ultimately determines the values, ethics and culture that pertains in any organisation.

Both books quote Sir John Harvey-Jones who, in his book *The Company Chairman*,[3] says:

> If a company is successful it is due to the efforts of everyone in it, but if it fails it is because of the failure of the board. If the board fails it is the responsibility of the chairman, notwithstanding the collective responsibility of everyone. Despite this collective responsibility, it is on the chairman's shoulders that the competition and the performance of that supreme directing body depends.

In one of our catch-ups, we discussed Zivit's experience in working with organisations on values and ethical issues. It became clear that, as she had originally suggested in her PhD thesis, the matter of values and ethics in strategic thinking and strategy implementation is a very real one that is impacted by national culture and institutional environment. She noted that this is particularly the case for Western companies from the 'developed world' that operate in the markets of developing and emerging economies.

Accordingly, it became obvious that a new work was indicated – one which focused on the ethical leadership role of boards and the relationship between the letter of the law and the spirit of the law, which becomes apparent when values and ethics overlie legislative requirements.

Our approach to this work was twofold. First, we interviewed a range of chairpersons in Australia, New Zealand and the United States (many of whom sit on boards governing companies in many other countries) in order to ascertain the values and ethical issues that they confront and their methods of dealing with these. Our interviewees come from a variety of companies: public, private, not-for-profit (NFP) and government. The sample included large organisations as well as small and medium-sized enterprises (SMEs).

One common theme which emerged from the interviews was the conflicting means of handling ethical matters and the tension between the concepts of law and ethics. On the one hand, most interviewees stated that ethics is above the law. You can follow the letter of the law, but still behave unethically. They stressed the importance of being ethical and not just adhering to the legislation as a key principle for strategic advantage. On the other hand, the majority of the interviewees argued that in order to dismiss a director from the board, the director's behaviour must have been illegal and unlawful. They feel that they cannot dismiss a director for unethical conduct, if the behaviour was still within legal boundaries. This is only one example of the tension between law and ethics; an ongoing confusion affecting many organisations that the ethics kaleidoscopes presented in this book are aiming to resolve.

Second, this qualitative research, using a grounded theory methodology, was then complemented by case studies that could demonstrate how the application (or non-application) of the values and ethics determined by the board impacted on organisational performance. The result is a book which – by demonstrating that operating in a way that inculcates strong positive values and a high ethical standard can bring about and maintain high performance – we hope will stimulate discussion and lead to better corporate governance through improved leadership.

This book is structured in two parts. The first part provides the conceptual background to the issue of ethics in organisations. The second part elaborates on the practical ethical dilemmas that boards deal with, providing insights into how to gain strategic advantage from ethical leadership.

Part I explains the major concepts which influence the ethical dilemmas that boards deal with. Here, we explore the issues of values, ethics as an overall concept, organisational culture in general and the complex topic of leadership. Each concept is developed using theoretical frameworks and practical examples.

Chapter 1 covers the concept of values and their relevance to every organisation. Chapter 2 then explains the concept of ethics and its connection to values. Next, Chapter 3 demonstrates how the actual practices of values and ethics in the workplace (rather than a company's stated policies) create the organisational culture, upon which employees base their decision making and behaviours. This chapter looks both at national and organisational culture. We start the section by explaining the relationships between culture, values and ethics. We then move on to discuss the challenges that boards are facing in managing culture and ethics – across national borders and within the organisation. The conclusion of the section is that, when managed correctly, ethics can provide organisations with an important strategic advantage.

We close the first part of the book by explaining what seems to be obvious – who is responsible for ethics in every organisation. Chapter 4 is all about leadership and why leaders need to proactively take ownership and model ethical decisions and behaviours.

While both parts of the book provide many examples and citations from our research, the second part is focused on practical insights into the board's role in corporate ethics. Chapter 5 presents the macro environment within which the board operates to resolve its many ethical dilemmas and challenges. Whereas society has undergone dramatic changes, the governance environment is lagging behind and finding it hard to adapt to these changes and progress. Ethical issues are then perceived as primary reasons for the fall of many global companies, coupled with the lack of proactive changes to the board's operating framework.

Chapter 6 looks at the micro (intra-company) ethical areas that boards deal with and presents the ethics kaleidoscope (the various lenses through which the issue of ethics can be viewed), a framework we developed to support better ethical decision making. The kaleidoscope includes five main lenses, or areas, for boards to look at on a regular basis. We call it a kaleidoscope since, when you turn your view from one lens to another, you get to see a different picture of the organisation and its ethical system and operation. Furthermore, the strength of diversity of thought in the boardroom comes into play when different people see the picture differently while looking through the same lens. Sharing their views and discussing the situation help directors to better govern. We came up with the idea of the kaleidoscope since, when asked about the role of boards in corporate ethics, it was apparent that most interviewees looked at ethics through one lens only, while ignoring other important ethical aspects.

Finally, we move to consider ways in which boards can be more effective in exemplifying the behaviour of individuals in an organisation that seeks to operate in an ethical manner. In Chapter 7 we gathered all the recommendations suggested by our interviewees and developed them into the kaleidoscope checklist, which boards can use to ensure they focus mindfully on ethics. This chapter provides recommendations from chairpersons about how to govern ethics and ensure that the board is not only responding to crises, but is proactively managing and gaining a sustainable strategic advantage from ethics. We hope that this chapter will encourage further discussion about the role of boards in ethics and how a group of people that meets, normally, on a monthly basis can actually not only know what is going on in the organisation – culturally and ethically – but also navigate the organisation's ethics for sustainable success.

Our research revealed that chairpersons typically look at ethics from one point of view only – reputation or marketing or research, etc. By developing the ethics kaleidoscope we hope to extend the way in which directors deal with ethics and make the concept less 'fluffy' and more tangible, easier to work with.

We hope you enjoy the book and look forward to receiving your feedback.

Notes

1 Gower Publication Limited, 2012.
2 Gower Publication Limited, 2013.
3 Director Books, UK, 1995.

Anecdotes from interviews

We decided to open the book in an unconventional way and, rather than explain the ethical problem theoretically, present a few anecdotes from interviews. These anecdotes illustrate how wide and varied the ethical dilemmas facing boards are.

Why do I care about ethics? I don't know if I have any values, I am interested in risk. I have an atheist view of ethics. It is all about the risk management. Do I care about having GMO in the wheat in my food? No! But I raise it at the board meeting, because it becomes a big issue in the media. I am interested in the risk mitigation point of view, not if it is healthy or not.

What do you do if the board makes a decision that you voted against because it is unethical in your view? It's a higher level of problem than a financial problem.

I caught the CEO lying. It took me two years to expose him. No one else in the board supported me. I could never get a straightforward answer from him and every part of my intuition indicated that he is lying. But the other directors said 'He is such a nice guy, what's your problem?'. You can't do anything based on intuition only, so I forced a restructure that included promotion of a few top executives. Those who have complied with him so far and didn't disclose to the board what is really going on all of the sudden had responsibilities and started talking about all the breaches that happened there behind the board's back.

Intuition ... I am looking at the behaviours at the table ... I joined an NFP board and had an intuition that there is something going on with the Chairman's behaviour. 'You are trying to convince yourself that they are not being unethical'. Sometimes, nobody has the guts to say something, because you don't want to be offensive to anyone. My intuition was right, but it took me too long to move on the issue.

Once you sit on many boards, it gives you the confidence to handle that, it's experience on boards.

The new CEO of XX Corp was a yes-man to the board. The whole OHS went down – they cut head count and training. Thereafter the big issue happened due to H&S. Now, these days, they advertise on TV that they have changed. They have more people and all the team is trained on OHS, so they are looking to gain customers' confidence.

A couple of interviewees reported that when they brought unethical behaviours to the board, the board stopped working with them.

At the core of all these short anecdotes hide the two important roles of the board – governance and leadership. Boards need not only to govern, but also to lead the ethics of the organisation. This book looks into the dilemmas that beset these roles and provides a framework within which directors can work.

Part I

The ethical context of governance

1 Values

Values are shared abstract ideas, implicit or explicit, that serve as guiding standards to actions, evaluation of situations, events, behaviours and people. Values influence our thoughts, feelings and actions in an unconscious manner. They provide guidance in analysing situations (what is rational for us is a consequence of our values). One of the important roles of values is in shaping our ethics and ethical decision making.

Values, or knowledge, that are shared by members of a certain group and influence their behaviours, are called norms. This knowledge helps in predicting behaviours of others in different situations.[1] Important norms are designed to protect society (for example, opposing murder or supporting elderly parents), less important norms cover behaviours such as manners and speech.

Unlike the motivation to conform to formal rules and regulations, the motivation to conform to social norms stems from the fear of the reaction of others in cases of deviation from these norms. According to Sunder, conformity to norms is also seen as a moral or ethical obligation. People obey and enforce a norm, because they internalise the norm in such a way that it becomes part of their preferences.

In other words, values are emotionally loaded beliefs that can change over time. Of course, these values are primarily individual and personal but there are always overlaps among people and in virtually any and every grouping of people there are significant quantities of shared values. Values reflect our world view and they frame our approach to ethics. In turn, our combined demonstration of ethics in any organisation leads to the evolution of an organisation's culture and, eventually, it is the culture of the organisation that dictates the behaviour which determines how the organisation is perceived by others.

This is illustrated in Figure 1.

Figure 1 From values come behaviours

However, despite the term 'values' being freely bandied around, the concept is really quite complex.

In the years 1981–1993, Australia experienced its greatest ever rise and fall of many big-name businesses, with their failures having significant follow-on effects, not just in the Australian economy but internationally as well. The legacy of just 20 of these is a cost to their investors of around 16.5 billion Australian dollars while their costs to the banks and related financial services organisations was in excess of 28 billion Australian dollars[2] – and this at a time when the Australian dollar was valued at a significantly higher rate than was the US dollar. Despite the protestations of many at the time, a financial disaster of this magnitude need not have occurred and it certainly was not simply the result of the behaviour of a relatively few isolated 'cowboys'. The faults were systemic – and they related to values and ethics.

Trevor Sykes, a widely respected financial journalist, investigated many of these collapses for his book *The Bold Riders* and his data make it clear that a key reason for these failures was that many of the auditors, financiers, corporate boards and regulators involved had failed to exercise good corporate governance. They knew the law and they knew what they should be doing but, for a variety of reasons, either they failed to act appropriately or they ensured that strict adherence to the letter of the law was observed but they ignored any breaches of the spirit of the law.

In the 1987 movie, *Wall Street*, Gordon Gekko uses the now well-known aphorism 'Greed is Good' to justify his actions in making money by any means possible in order to further his desires for wealth, power and influence. The 'bold riders' of whom Sykes wrote certainly believed this and, in the pursuit of their wealth objectives, what many consider to be ethical behaviour was the last thing on their minds.

In 1997, Bob Garratt, a consultant advising on director development and strategic thinking, published *The Fish Rots From The Head*[3] in which he makes the point that many directors lose sight of the fact that, legally, they are accountable to the company itself as a legal personality. He points out that most directors see themselves as representatives of such parties as shareholders or lenders and so tend to focus on what is good for these parties rather than on what is best for the company per se in both the short and long term. A direct consequence of this is that, far too often, doing what is legal becomes conflated with doing what is ethical and this can have serious adverse implications for the company to which they are actually accountable. He specifically refers to Australia's experience of the 1990s in this discussion.

In discussing issues impacting the running of successful companies, it is not uncommon to hear people say that the principal responsibility of boards and managers is to maximise profit so that shareholders reap high dividends from their stockholdings. That this is a naive premise can be quickly demonstrated by considering the relationship between risk and reward. The truth is that, for both short-term and long-term sustainability and success, an appropriate balance between risk and reward needs to be struck. A high level of risk in some business ventures may well have the potential to yield extremely high profits – but the downside may be total collapse of the business. For this reason, responsible boards and managers focus far more on profit optimisation that has the potential to result in wealth maximisation. Taking a more manageable degree of risk may result in lower levels of profit (in both the short and long term) but, because of good governance and sound management practices, the potential for wealth maximisation is optimised.

It was the quest for profit maximisation that drove Sykes' 'bold riders'[4] and which led to the excesses that characterised their operations. To them, 'wealth maximisation' was equated with 'profit maximisation'. Unfortunately, as Sykes makes clear, these same 'bold riders' had little difficulty in drawing their auditors, lawyers, banks and related financial institutions into the same quagmire. The contest became one of profit pursuit, regardless of whether or not there were appropriate business foundations or if the business was really sound. Dissenting voices were quickly hushed and, ultimately, no one had the cojones to point out that the emperor was without clothes.

If we believe the rhetoric, the collapse of the 'bold riders' and the collateral damage experienced by the professional services, legal entities, banks and financial services organisations provided a salutary lesson that drove the emphasis back to wealth maximisation. But, as Andrew Main made clear in two much later books,[5] the problematic patterns of behaviour clearly identified by Sykes continued throughout the rest of the twentieth century.

In addition, towards the end of the 1990s we had the 'dot com' boom and bust and, in the first decades of the twenty-first century we have experienced the re-emergence of an emphasis on profit maximisation that, in a significant number of companies, has manifested itself as a 'do anything it takes' mentality to winning business in both developed and developing economies. Over the past 15 years, in Australia alone serious questions have been raised about the activities of the Australian Wheat Board in relation to trade with Iraq, of various construction companies in relation to international infrastructure deals and of a banknote printing business, which has strong connections to the Reserve Bank of Australia, in relation to the obtaining of contracts to produce polymer notes for foreign countries. At the same time, in the United Kingdom, there has been the phone hacking scandal affecting News Corporation. Then, in 2007, the USA saw the start of the disastrous global financial crisis, which reactivated the 'greed is good' approach and enabled a relatively small number of people across the world to make large fortunes (in part thanks to Government bail-outs) while many small investors lost everything.

And so we could continue. With monotonous regularity it seems that those involved in corporate governance and corporate management operate in ways that call into question the veracity of any stated values and ethics that are purported to underpin both their goals and their modus operandi.

In the commerce degrees at the Australian School of Business, University of New South Wales (UNSW), the subject of values and ethics is introduced as a compulsory area of study for undergraduate students. In 2015, one of the assignments related to the rationale for organisations to be seen as good corporate citizens through the implementation of corporate social responsibility (CSR). Most students quickly ascertained that, although there were arguments both for and against CSR, the general consensus was that there were sound economic reasons underlying an organisation's CSR activity. But when the students compared CSR activity in Australia with that outside Australia there was some amazement across the student body to discover that, at the very time they were doing the study, in the United States, New York was being brought to a standstill due to low-paid workers having to fight for an increase in their minimum hourly rate of US$8.90 – well below any form of living wage – and that, in New Zealand, it had been made legal for organisations to offer contracts to casual staff in which there are no minimum hours mandated and in which all the power rests with the employer. The overwhelming feedback from the students was that exploitation in the quest for profit maximisation indicated serious deficiencies in the values and ethics of those responsible for corporate governance and corporate management. While acknowledging that history indicates students are often idealistic, it can also be argued that values are evolving from one generation to another and it seems that this generation (called Gen Y) has a significantly higher or more developed environmental and social conscience than is found in much of the practice of conservative corporate governance.

Concurrent with this study by UNSW commerce students was an Australian Government enquiry into the behaviour of international corporations that seek to minimise their taxation liabilities by shifting profits away from Australia to those jurisdictions with the lowest corporate tax rates. Based on statements from the highest political levels in Australia, the United Kingdom and some other major economies, it seems possible that, in the not too distant future, there might be renewed examination of not only the legal basis for such transfers but also in relation to the value systems and ethics that underpin such practices of corporations.

The Davos Conference in Switzerland in 2016 focused even more attention on this shifting of profits and, indirectly, on the ethics involved by publishing a report by Oxfam[6] which pointed out:

> Just 62 people, 53 of them men, own as much wealth as the poorest half of the entire world population and the richest 1 per cent own more than the other 99 per cent put together, anti-poverty charity Oxfam said on Monday.
>
> The Oxfam report suggests that global inequality has reached levels not seen in over a century.
>
> Last year, the organisation has calculated, 62 individuals had the same wealth as 3.5 billion people, or the bottom half of humanity. The wealth of those 62 people has risen 44 per cent, or more than half a trillion dollars, over the past five years, while the wealth of the bottom half has fallen by over a trillion.
>
> 'Far from trickling down, income and wealth are instead being sucked upwards at an alarming rate,' the report says.
>
> It points to a 'global spider's web' of tax havens that ensures wealth stays out of reach of ordinary citizens and governments, citing a recent estimate that $US7.6 trillion ($A11.08 trillion) of individual wealth – more than the combined economies of Germany and the UK – is currently held offshore.

That same newspaper article also makes the point that:

> Politicians and business leaders gathering in the Swiss Alps this week face an increasingly divided world, with the poor falling further behind the super-rich and political fissures in the United States, Europe and the Middle East running deeper than at any time in decades.

In *Delivering High Performance: The Third Generation Organisation*[7] the point is made that it is the Chairman of an organisation who is ultimately responsible for everything that occurs within the organisation and for everything that the organisation stands for and does. This includes the values and ethics espoused by and practised throughout the organisation.

One of the things we know about values is that they can change over time. This was discussed in *Leaders: Diamonds or Cubic Zirconia*[8] when considering the issue of how education and life experience can bring about a difference in the way we think about things and, over time, can mean that the values driving our behaviour can change and develop.

Third Generation Leadership and the Locus of Control: Knowledge, Change and Neuroscience[9] discusses the work of Professor Clare Graves as it is expounded by Don Beck and Chris Cowan.[10] Graves argued that people's value systems (or 'memes') are able to change as they mature and their values acumen develops. Graves argues that the value memes fall into a series of tiers (similar in many ways to octaves in music) in which value memes are repeated at different levels. At the first level, when in any meme, a person has what could be called a monochromatic view – at any one time they are totally immersed in that meme and are unable to see beyond it. At the second level it becomes possible to see things in a more complex fashion and to recognise when and where each meme is appropriate – what could be described as a polychromatic view. In Graves' model, the memes in each level can be described as: survival, family or tribe, power or aggression, authority or law, excellence or competition, socially responsible. All people progress through some of the levels but there is no internal or external compulsion to automatically proceed. Values acumen can develop as a person discovers that world views and behaviours that were previously appropriate are no longer sufficient and that change may be required. At this stage, a person has the choice of maintaining their values acumen at its current stage or moving to the next level. Earlier memes never disappear but they contribute to a more rich and complex set of world views and behaviours by remaining accessible along with the new meme. Beck and Cowan argue that the dominant memes in today's world are a combination of power or aggression, authority or law, excellence or competition in their first tier format. Only a relatively small number of people and organisations will proceed to the meme of social responsibility and considerably fewer will then make the step-shift from the first to the second tier. The result is that exhortations to universal implementation of comprehensive CSR initiatives will be neither understood nor accepted by the majority – they will be seen as being in conflict with what is perceived to be 'the real world'. (This 'real world' argument is explored by Caroline Flammer,[11] who demonstrates that shareholders are positive to CSR initiatives only up to a certain point. She argues that, at least in relation to environmental CSR, corporate social responsibility is a resource with decreasing marginal returns. She points out that there comes a point where the costs of CSR outweigh any economic benefit to an organisation. For those seeking profit maximisation, this becomes a powerful argument against CSR expenditure and any suggestion that it could lead to profit optimisation.)

Graves' framework enables us to understand why it is that we experience phenomena such as Australia's 'bold riders' in the 1980s, the 'dot com' boom and bust, the more recent global financial crisis and the all-too-common practices of paying a high level of remuneration to people at the top of organisations while complaining bitterly about any increase in remuneration to those lacking in positional power. From an idealistic perspective, such behaviour may be considered unethical but, interpreted in light of the dominant memes of those in positions of power and authority, it may be both totally understandable and probably 'ethical' behaviour. After all, if ethics is about what I 'ought' to do, then my dominant world view (my memes) will impact strongly on all my moral imperatives. My behaviour ethic, or what I ought to do, is always inextricably linked to my values – my emotionally loaded beliefs.

Some years ago, Stephen Covey confronted this issue of changes in values and resolved it by arguing that the focus should be on 'principles' rather than 'values'. Covey says, 'Principles, unlike values, are objective and external. They operate in obedience to natural laws, regardless of conditions. Values are subjective and internal'.[12] He sees these principles as being fairness, equity, justice, integrity, honesty and trust. Covey then argues that these principles lead to four life centres, which he nominates as security, guidance, power and wisdom, and states that these have both a personal and an organisational perspective. Covey says that, used positively, these four life centres become powerful forces for good but that using them negatively, through focusing on alternative or subsidiary centres, leads to exploitation and harm.

Despite criticism from some, Covey's argument is far more than a semantic distinction between 'principles' and 'values' and he makes a strong case for the primacy of principles. However, as Covey also makes clear, there can still be problems concerning the issue of personal commitment to principles and the exercise of good organisational management. How does one deal with the dissonance that arises from a perceived difference between what is said and what is done? How, also, does one deal with the dissonance that can arise from my behaviour in private and my behaviour in the corporate world? This is the very real concern that organisations face in relation to empowerment.

Third Generation Leadership and the Locus of Control[13] argues that the answer lies in empowerment that relies on personal accountability rather than on rigid controls and makes the point that, in order to hold someone accountable, it is imperative that he or she has all of the information necessary to make an informed decision that is in accord with the organisation's overall approach. If, as a director, executive or senior manager, I fail to ensure that full and frank information is available, as and when required, to those who make decisions, then the fault is mine – not theirs – when inappropriate decisions are made. If I am serious about empowerment then, sometimes, I must take the risk of sharing information that, in an environment based on tight controls, I would not normally share. Because, in these cases, there is always a risk that such information might be misused, it is not surprising that empowerment is more frequently found in rhetoric rather than in practice – and that is true whether or not the primary focus is on principles or values.

The advocates of profit maximisation tend to concentrate on tight control with minimal sharing of information that has the potential to be used in a manner contrary to a manager's intent. As Sykes[14] makes clear, the 'bold riders' tightly controlled the disclosure of information within their empires so as to minimise the risk that awkward questions might be asked and unpalatable truths might be revealed. What they disclosed might be 'the truth' (or at least a version of it) but it was never 'the whole truth and nothing but the truth'. Profit optimisation and wealth maximisation – not just for a select few but for everyone – requires empowerment. And we have a long way to go before empowerment becomes 'the norm'. It is a very big step from the combination of power or aggression, authority or law, excellence or competition in Beck and Cowan's[15] first tier format to even the spiral's next stage of being socially responsible!

So, if 'values' are not absolute, what is the case with 'ethics'?

Notes

1 Sunder, S. (2005) Minding our manners: Accounting as social norms, *The British Accounting Review*, pp. 1–21.
2 Sykes, T. (1996). *The Bold Riders*, (2nd edn), Allen & Unwin, St Leonards, Australia.
3 Garratt, B. (1997) *The Fish Rots from the Head: The Crisis in our Boardrooms: Developing the Crucial Skills of the Competent Director*, HarperCollins, London.
4 Sykes (1996) op. cit.
5 Main, A. (2003) *Other People's Money: The Complete Story of the Extraordinary Collapse of HIH*, HarperCollins, Sydney and (2005) *Rivkin Unauthorised: The Meteoric Rise and Tragic Fall of an Unorthodox Money Man*, HarperCollins, Sydney.
6 Available at http://www.smh.com.au/world/worlds-richest-1-per-cent-own-more-than-the-other-99-per-cent-put-together-oxfam-report-20160118-gm8nxl#ixzz3xeCA45CO [20 July 2016].
7 Long, D. G. (2013) *Delivering High Performance: The Third Generation Organisation*, 2013, Gower, Farnham, UK.

8 Long, D. G. (1998) *Leaders: Diamonds or Cubic Zirconia – Asia Pacific Leaders on Leadership*, CLS, Sydney, reissued as an e-book 2012, Blurb Books (blurb.com).

9 Long, D. G. (2012) *Third Generation Leadership and the Locus of Control: Knowledge, Change and Neuroscience*, Gower, Farnham, UK.

10 Beck, D. and Cowan, C. (1996) *Spiral Dynamics: Mastering Values, Leadership and Change*, Blackwell, USA.

11 Flammer, C. (2013) Corporate social responsibility and shareholder reaction: The environmental awareness of investors, *Academy of Management Journal*, Vol. 56, No. 3, June, pp. 758–781.

12 Covey, S. R. (1991) *Principle Centred Leadership*, Fireside, New York, p. 19.

13 Long (2012) op. cit.

14 Sykes (1996) op. cit.

15 Beck and Cowan (1996) op. cit.

2　Ethics

In 1997, Joseph Fletcher,[1] an Episcopalian clergyman in the United States, released a new version of his book on ethics.[2] Fletcher's argument was that the most ethical thing to do in any situation was to follow the path of implementing 'the greatest love' for the person or people involved. He was trying to find a middle road between the emphases of various approaches to ethics. His argument was that the emphasis should always be on the results – the outcome or consequences – of any action. In other words, assessments of whether or not an action is ethical can only be made by assessing the action in relation to its context.

Interestingly, the first edition of Fletcher's work was published at around the same time that Clare Graves was developing the concepts that Don Beck and Chris Cowan discuss in *Spiral Dynamics*.[3] A brief consideration of both concepts shows that there is some overlap of concepts. Graves argues that ethics must be considered in light of value memes while Fletcher argues that ethics must be considered in light of context. Both agree that there are no 'absolutes' and that assessment of what is or is not ethical is a complex rather than a simple matter.

As might be expected, these approaches have their genesis in traditional approaches on ethical versus unethical behaviour, although they may be expressed quite differently from their forebears. Traditional approaches can be loosely grouped into:

- Kantian ethics, based on the work of Immanuel Kant (a philosopher of the period 1724–1804), who argued that we should only act in the way we want others to act. This is based on actions of the individual and, in this approach, it tends to be that one's underlying intention is more important than any consequences. Of course, an ex post facto analysis can almost always be provided to justify the intent, no matter what has occurred.

- Utilitarianism – an approach that argues that the rightness or otherwise of our actions is determined by a comparative assessment of their consequences. This approach was developed by the philosophers Jeremy Bentham (1748–1832) and John Stuart Mill (1806–1873). Here, the consequences take precedence over the intent – an action is 'right' if it maximises the common or collective good. Of course, the question of fully determining the 'common' good may result in different answers that are dependent upon another range of factors.

- Universalism, which argues that there is only ever one 'right' set of behaviours regardless of the circumstances and the onus is on the individual to always behave 'correctly', despite any environmental or situational factors that may impact. This, of course, makes it easy for a person to determine the appropriateness of their actions but, as might be expected, it can set in train a process that may produce results which are vastly different from any theoretical constructs that underlie the theory. By considering ethics as universal, this approach omits the differences in national cultures and their influence on ethics. We know today that in different countries (and within countries) we have a variety of cultures and ethical systems.

- Relativism, which argues that there are no independent principles or standards for determining whether or not an action is 'right' and so no set of moral beliefs is more correct than any other. This approach virtually allows an individual or an existing culture to determine what is or is not appropriate, with the result that widely divergent actions may be considered appropriate within the same society or organisation. It is, of course, just a short step from this to the situation in which all consideration of ethics is purely a subjective judgement by an individual.

While Covey[4] argues for the primacy of principles over values for determining appropriate versus inappropriate behaviour, there seems to be some consensus that, at least in developed countries, ethical behaviour should consist of competing fairly and honestly, communicating truthfully, acting in a transparent manner and not harming others. Clearly, there is an overlap here with Covey's 'principles'. But are these what we see when we consider actual behaviour? How does this consensus on 'ethical' behaviour relate to such issues as:

- exploitation of labour in developing countries in order to enhance developed countries' profits;
- discrimination on the grounds of age, gender, sexual orientation, religious persuasion, colour, race, and so on;

- reducing quality in order to maximise profits;
- paying 'facilitation fees' to interested third parties in order to obtain contracts;
- threatening or actually inflicting violence or blackmail in order to achieve one's ends;
- failing to observe even reasonable (let alone minimum appropriate) health, safety and/or environmental safeguards in the conducting of business;
- focusing on short-term results in order to maximise personal benefits even when such a focus could endanger the long-term viability of an enterprise;
- acting in any way at all that could be considered by others as an 'end justifies the means' approach;
- while always telling 'the truth', omitting to tell all the truth and allowing others to act in accordance with misconceptions based on a lack of full information?

Many of these activities are, of course, illegal (at least in developed countries) but it doesn't prevent them from happening – very often with those involved performing all kinds of legal gymnastics to try to persuade critics that they are behaving in accordance with the letter of the law, even if it is possible that a moral line may have been crossed.

In April 2015, this issue of ethics was highlighted in Australia when David Thodey, the outgoing CEO of Telstra (Australia's largest supplier of telecommunication services), stated in a media interview:[5]

> I get paid a lot of money [and] my options, should they vest, are worth tens of millions of dollars. … But I can't sit here and defend my salary against all the guys who are out there working every day and I wouldn't try to.
>
> I think there's a real issue with income disparity between what an average person gets and some of the really big salaries.

As a quick read of the report will show, there was some backlash to this comment. People pointed out that he waited until his very last day in the job before raising the issue and at least one person queried the fact that Telstra, like most other companies, had different standards for assessing whether or not they could afford salary increments for executives compared with other staff. While 'ethics' per se was not mentioned, it was clear that a few people considered that at least the timing of Thodey's statement had some negative linkage to ethics.

This highlights the difficulty faced by CEOs and boards in relation to publically raising ethical issues. It is widely accepted that CEOs and boards have a primary responsibility to get the best possible return for their organisation's owners – the shareholders. If, during his or her tenure in the top job, a CEO raises the issue of being overpaid and, either implicitly or explicitly, indicates that more could be done to increase the remuneration of lower level staff, the floodgates to a torrent of pay increase claims are opened and that is likely to have a detrimental impact on stock prices as investors start to believe that dividends may reduce. The stock market is interested only in returns on investment and if there is a perception that these returns will reduce, then the company is usually savaged. The result is damaging to the owners and, regardless of their ethical intent, the CEO and/or board have failed in their legislated responsibility.

But sometimes both the ethical and legal issues are quite clear. Consider the case of James Hardie Industries.

James Hardie Industries was a major Australian manufacturing company that, starting in the 1930s, developed asbestos-based products. In 1964, management had evidence that asbestos had caused serious disease in some of its people and that they were at risk of developing mesothelioma – an extremely virulent form of lung cancer. However, the company did nothing until 1977 when it eventually included warning labels on these products and it was not until 1987 that they ceased production of all asbestos products. The following years saw a significant number of compensation claims and, in 2001, the company established a trust valued at $203 million[6] to fund all such claims. They stated that they had done this for the mutual benefit of claimants and shareholders and that the fund was fully funded. They then moved their headquarters to the Netherlands, where they would no longer be subject to Australian controls. By 2003, it was clear that the fund was not fully funded but the company refused to contribute any further money. This led to a Government enquiry in 2004. The enquiry found that the company had breached the Australian Corporations Act and the CEO and board faced possible criminal action. Eventually, the company agreed to guarantee compensation to all present and future claimants and set up a $4 billion fund.[7]

However, there are other cases where the situation is not quite so clear cut.

As a developed country, Australia has very specific laws relating to minimum wages and employment conditions for all workers. Australia also has a trade union movement (of which membership is voluntary) that actively works to ensure that these legal conditions are, at a minimum, adhered to and, ideally, exceeded. In the main, employers – at least all major employers – comply with these laws. However, there is a constant complaint by many employers that the cost of labour is too high and that, particularly in areas such as the service industries, agricultural products and mining, having to meet the legal minimum requirements makes businesses uncompetitive. In part to address these concerns, some years ago Australia passed legislation to enable temporary work visas to be issued, which allow for the employment of visitors to Australia for short periods under less restrictive conditions than normal Australian workplace conditions.

On Monday 4 May 2015, the Australian Broadcasting Corporation, in its programme 'Four Corners' ran an exposé showing that, under cost-reduction pressures from Australia's major supermarket chains, produce suppliers with contracts to these chains, were using a variety of legislative loopholes in order to employ people under conditions significantly below those that are mandated.[8] The ethical question relates to whether or not the supermarket chains have a moral responsibility to ensure that their local suppliers (who have a legal responsibility to adhere to Australian workplace conditions) are actually adhering to these conditions. Given that the Government has regulatory authorities specifically tasked with ensuring that correct working conditions are maintained, is it the supermarkets' responsibility to police the operations of their suppliers? Clearly, the supermarkets would argue that they are working to keep the cost of food at the lowest possible level for consumers and that it is up to the Government to police how the local suppliers run their businesses in order to remain profitable. As the report shows, there are many people who have a different view.

However, there is a difference between this situation in Australia and the cases of developed country companies manufacturing and/or buying in developing countries that utilise sweatshop conditions. Because developing countries do not have the legislative and policing facilities found in developed countries, the only means to ensure that employees are not exploited is for the developed economy companies to do appropriate due diligence and to monitor working conditions in the facilities their suppliers use. In such instances, as many highly publicised cases have shown, there is clearly an ethical imperative for companies from developed countries to behave correctly.

In 2015, we interviewed the chairs of various companies in Australia, New Zealand and the United States. With their varied directorship roles, the research covered over 100 companies. While all agreed that ethics was important, it was clear that for many of these chairpersons – all of them very influential men and women in their wider communities – acting ethically was seen as acting in accordance with legal requirements. For them, it seemed as though 'acting ethically' and 'acting legally' were close to synonymous. Those who saw ethics as above the law were faced with many questions of how to define and lead ethical behaviour in the organisation and inside the boardroom. While illegal activities are easy to define and there are rules determining how to manage them, it becomes a greyer area when facing ethical issues. For example, external audits proactively look for illegal irregularities, while ethical considerations remain in the background and in most cases are aired only after an event has got of control. Directors of big corporations agree that it often takes a good two years for the board to find out about an ethical issue. At that point in time, the board needs to deal with damage control and this, rather than the ethical behaviour or norm that caused the problem, tends to be the focus of attention. The result is that, all too often, the underlying ethical issue receives little, if any, real attention.

And here, perhaps, is the crux of the problem confronting organisations today. While agreeing that ethics is all about what I 'ought' to do, far too often we fail to distinguish between what I 'ought' to do from a *legal* perspective and what I 'ought' to do from a *moral* perspective. From a legal perspective there was no issue with James Hardie Industries moving their operations to the Netherlands, but from a moral perspective a different conclusion may be drawn. From a legal perspective, outsourcing operations to sweat shops in a developing country may be justified, but it was people considering the issue from a moral perspective who drew attention to this activity and who generated some change.

Ray Anderson, a successful US entrepreneur running a billion-dollar company operating in 110 countries, was faced with the possibility of losing sales because of the environmental concerns of some customers. A question from one of his executives regarding how this could be addressed, forced him to confront the dilemma of what I 'ought' to do from a *legal* perspective and what I 'ought' to do from a *moral* perspective. In his book *The Power of One Good Question*[9] he describes how his company, Interface, then made the transition from being a company that was 100 per cent compliant with every legal requirement to being a world leader in environmentally friendly practices that went far beyond anything required by authorities. On their website, Interface set out the original vision propounded in 1997 and, in his book, Anderson shows how he has found that doing 'what I "ought" to do from a *moral* perspective' has presented new opportunities and enabled organisational growth that he never imagined. Their website states:

> Interface's 1994 mid-course correction steered the company away from the typical take-make-waste business model toward one that's renewable, cyclical, and benign.
>
> That Interface is about change was clear from its inception, when Ray Anderson staked his career on the unprecedented concept of

modular carpet tile. Two decades later, in 1994, Ray had his legend-ary 'spear in the chest' epiphany. He shook the foundations of the petroleum-intensive carpet manufacturing industry by declaring that Interface was committed to becoming the world's first environmen-tally sustainable – and, ultimately, restorative – company.

A new focus emerged: to radically redesign processes and products and to pioneer new technologies and systems that reduce or eliminate waste and harmful emissions while increasing the use of renewable materials and energy sources. Interface established its Mission Zero® promise to eliminate any negative impact the company has on the environment by 2020 and, supported by our entrepreneurial spirit, we're well on our way to achieving it.

'If we're successful, we'll spend the rest of our days harvesting yester-year's carpets and other petrochemically derived products, and recycling them into new materials; and converting sunlight into energy; with zero scrap going to the landfill and zero emissions into the ecosystem. And we'll be doing well ... very well ... by doing good. That's the vision.'

Ray Anderson, 1997

But not all of the 'what ought I to do?' questions are as simple.

At the end of 2014, several groups called for the Royal Children's Hospital (RCH) in Melbourne, Victoria to drop its contract with the McDonald's fast food chain, saying it is similar to a cancer hospital supporting tobacco.[10] While there were many who agreed with this opinion, others took a different stance. One of the RCH Board mem-bers said in the interview: 'a kid is dying from cancer – who am I to say that he cannot have McDonalds at the hospital?'

There is another recent, famous case in Australia–Indonesia relations in which a number of Australians travelled to Bali with the intention of traf-ficking drugs. They were apprehended and brought to trial in Bali and the two ringleaders were subsequently executed by firing squad while the others received lengthy prison sentences. This 'Bali 9' case (as it came to be known) started with the father of one of the offenders approaching the Australian Federal Police to ask for help in preventing his son from leaving the country and committing a crime. The Australian police ignored his plea to stop the son's departure, passed this information on to the Indonesian authorities and allowed the crime to be committed despite knowing that the penalty in Indonesia would probably be death. The Australian Federal Police acted within the law, but did they act ethically given the father's appeal for help?

A third example is the board of a major telecommunications com-pany that realised the level of complaints was not normal and it became clear that something was amiss in relation to customer satisfaction. Although the board received data about complaints at every meeting, actual satisfaction seemed to be declining rather than improving. In addition, the overall impressions that the directors received from their personal interactions with family and friends were different from what the board was being told. They then realised that the board was not receiving the right information about customer service and they took steps to both find out the reason for this and to correct the situation.

In another company, the chairman found out that some investors and shareholders were actively trying to undermine the company, in order to reduce its value.

The board of a Superannuation Fund was looking into the question of 'to what extent do we take into consideration non-financial factors in investment'. Do we invest in companies that damage the environment? One of the triggers for this question was when a third party found out that they invested in tobacco companies (whose shares did very well) and pressure was applied to divest the company of these shares. The directors were faced with a dilemma: 'We need to take care of the investment and profit of our members. Should we invest in tobacco companies or companies that employ children?'

Or consider the case of zoos. Is it ethical to keep animals in captivity? We do it both for conservation purposes and to allow people to connect with them and care for them. While there may be no issue concerning the conservation aspect of zoos, there may well be ethical issues surrounding the keeping of animals primarily for the purposes of entertainment.

Banks exist in a constant state of conflicting interests. This, of course, becomes obvious when, as they did prior to the 2008 financial crash, many made huge amounts of money from financing sub-prime deals. But it is also evident when people are issued with credit cards which have limits that are far beyond an individual's ability to service. Then, when people fail to pay their balance, they are charged fees and percentages which provide significant amounts of banking profits. To what extent does a bank really want to notify them of the true extent of their indebtedness? Graham Hand, a one-time senior banker, raised issues such as this in his 2001 book *Naked Among Cannibals*.[11] He pointed out that, in his experience, the making of a profit out of customers always took precedence over any ethical considerations. He draws attention to the fact that, in 1993, the combined net profits of Australia's 'Big Four' banks was $1.9 billion while in the year 2000 those same banks returned a net profit of $9.4 billion through a focus on profit and share price at the expense of their customers. The fact that not too much may have changed since 2000 is reflected in a report found in the *Canberra Times* on 20 January 2016.[12] In this report a journalist, Clancy Yeates, discusses the move by some of Australia's major banks to emphasise ethics as part of their competitive advantage. While Yeates acknowledges that this might be because of a desire to improve behaviour, he goes on to argue that this is really a pre-emptive strike by the banks against more intrusive regulations. He points out that some banks allow a culture in which there are instances 'where people working in the financial markets responded to an ethical dilemma by doing whatever they could get away with, rather than what was right'. Yeates concludes with a call for real cultural change to take place so that ethical behaviour is found at every level and in every interaction.

Then there was the CEO who, after hearing that the company was about to be wound up and despite instructions from the global chairman not to make any increases without his prior approval, gave salary increases and promised bonuses in writing to his employees. He maintained his reputation locally and is loved, although what he did was, by some considerations, possibly illegal and strictly unethical.

The question 'What ought I to do?' can elicit some quite terrifying conundrums for those who ask it – which is probably why so many people prefer to avoid the question. Of course, others, who consciously lead by modelling their ethical system, see this question as their personal guide for making any decision – big or small. Organisations frequently face ethical paradoxes that stem from cross-cultural business. For example, what is perceived as good parenting in one culture, can be perceived as child abuse in another.

We will discuss this cross-cultural aspect in more detail in the next chapter.

The issue of ethical research

At universities in Australia and in most of the Western world at least, almost any research that is proposed must be approved by an ethics committee. The purpose of this is to ensure that any conflicts of interest are identified and acknowledged, as well as making sure that everything done is in accordance with the highest ethical protocols. Most commercial operations do not have this safeguard. Much of the material released to support advertising claims seems to come from companies which use research that is paid for by a certain industry or interest groups and hence is biased. Yet, in many cases, they do not reveal this information.

It has become commonplace today for advertisements to feature someone wearing a white research coat or claiming to be 'Doctor' who then goes on to make claims along the lines of 'university studies prove ...' or 'research studies prove ...' without giving any further details, including who actually did the research, where the research was done, how the sample was chosen, what checks were carried out to confirm the validity of data, what (if any) peer reviews were done, and where the specific report can be accessed so that independent judgements can be made.

In a discussion with a heart surgeon, he claimed that he works in the least ethical system in the world. His argument was based on what he is seeing on a day-to-day basis in terms of:

- how medicine is being marketed to doctors (giving them presents, sending them to free conferences overseas and reporting only on corroborative research findings, without mentioning the research that failed or had mixed reports);
- his colleagues that select patients on whom they operate privately (he claimed that some doctors tend not to accept patients that need complicated surgeries, in order to keep their own success rate and reputation high and/or not to have to be called back to the hospital after hours).

Personal ethics vs corporate ethics

As we have tried to illustrate, the board's role is in constant ethical conflict. It acts on behalf of a non-human ethical system (the corporation that needs to live forever). The directors' role is to ensure that the organisation can live forever.

However, at the same time, the directors have self-interests and/or see themselves as representing shareholders who may have short-term interests. Is it ethical to act on a short-term duty to the shareholder if that action undermines the long-term sustainability of the organisation? How ethical are situations where the shareholder is stronger than the corporation? As some chairs said at interview:

We operate in an unethical system, however the only unethical issues we face are human based, not structural (related to the corporate governance system).

Companies are aggregations of people's behaviors. Some owners of companies adopt 'shadowy' practices.

Ethics require a moral judgement; companies cannot make moral judgement.

It is the human ethical practices then that shape the corporate ethics and board members find this challenging. As one of the leading chairpersons in Australia said: 'how do you distinguish personal ethics from corporate ethics? You cannot control everybody all the time'.

Corporate ethics is acting in a way that is mutually beneficial to both parties and which contributes to sustainable success. In 2011, Professor Rebecca Henderson and Research Associate Frederik Nellemann of Harvard University published a case study on Unilever's commitment to a new 'sustainable living plan' that would transform the way it interacted with its suppliers in developing countries.[13] This study quotes the CEO of Unilever, Paul Polman, arguing that such actions as educating children and ethical growing and harvesting of raw products in developing countries would help to create a more desirable world overall. In addition, such action would help to ensure the future and the growth of Unilever itself. Reading the case study makes it clear that, to a great extent, this action was driven by the personal value systems and ethics of Polman himself, but clearly there was a congruity between Polman's values and those that Unilever itself saw as being appropriate drivers for its business.

This issue of personal vs corporate ethics was also raised by one of the chairmen we interviewed. This person was chairman of a major national company (a listed public entity) and he mentioned how, in the quest for growth through lateral acquisition, they had acquired a highly profitable business operation even though one of the directors had serious ethical concerns, given that the new acquisition's operations, while totally legal, appeared to be in conflict with espoused values. He pointed out that, in the quest for growth and profit, the ethical issues were put to one side and were not allowed to influence the acquisition.

In the Unilever case, clearly personal values and organisational values combined to bring about a highly ethical approach. In the second case, when it came to the crunch, neither personal values nor espoused organisational values were allowed to impact on potential profits.

There is a further issue here concerning the question of 'personal ethics' and that relates to why people take positions on boards. In the for-profit sector this is not so much of an issue because in these organisations directors tend to receive significant monetary fees, together with some protection in terms of insurance cover in the event of litigation, but in the not-for-profit sector (at least in Australia) the situation is quite different. In Australia, directors of not-for-profit organisations (NFPs) are appointed on a pro bono basis and, although legitimate expenses can be reimbursed, no directors' fees per se are permitted. This naturally begs the question as to why someone would take on a job that can still incur personal liability while not receiving any reward for the risk involved.

Clearly, some people take on this role for purely altruistic reasons. In the main, this would be true of those for whom there is no possible compensatory personal gain in terms of, say, reputation or wider career advancement. But for others the rationale is not so clear – perhaps not even to the individual concerned. And if the real rationale is hidden even from the person involved, then how does this impact on their exercise of ethics as part of good corporate governance.

Some years ago, Doug was providing consultancy services for a very well-established, medium-sized NFP with revenues around $10 million and employing over 100 staff. Just prior to Doug's involvement the chair had become aware of funds going missing and an initial (very covert) internal investigation implicated at least the finance manager and possibly the CEO. The chair then faced a dilemma. On the one hand, there was the legal issue of safeguarding possible evidence and initiating police involvement and, on the other hand, was the need to maintain confidence in this organisation from both the Government (who were providers of significant funds) and the public at large (who both used the organisation's services and also donated large amounts of money). The ethical issue was not about involving the police and notifying all appropriate authorities. The ethical issue related to the timing of such actions. Of course, had the chair decided not to contact the police and the other relevant authorities but, instead, had decided to cover up the incident and allow the offending parties to escape any form of formal investigation and, in this instance, criminal charges, then a totally different set of ethical (and probably legal) questions arise. As it happens, in this case, the actions taken by the chair enabled the organisation to deal with the problem in an open and effective manner and they helped set it up to be the very successful ($A30+ million) NFP that it is today.

More recently, Doug encountered a different ethical issue involving NFPs. He was asked by a small NFP to help them decide their future. Given changes to government funding protocols, it was clear that the organisation had a very limited future as a stand-alone entity. It became obvious that the only real chance of survival lay in merging with a larger organisation with a similar ethos but not offering the same services. Two such organisations (both in the same geographic region and both with impeccable reputations) were suggested as potential partners and both were very receptive to the possibility. At the annual general meeting (AGM), Doug presented the report and the meeting decided the board should investigate both possible options and then report back to a special general meeting concerning their recommendation. During the meeting, however, it became was clear that there was some bias in favour of one of the contenders. Later, despite the AGM resolution, it became obvious that the board had only seriously considered one contender and, coincidentally, that there may have been a connection between this contender and an influential board member. At no point in the AGM was this possible connection ever made public knowledge. In the for-profit world, this possible conflict of interest would probably result in some subsequent action by other board members or management. In the not-for-profit world, especially given the small nature of the organisation involved, it will probably remain uninvestigated and be considered inconsequential.

The point being made here is that the issue of ethics is not confined to large organisations nor to for-profit organisations. Corruption of one sort or another impacts every sector of society and every type of organisation. Ethical behaviour is the responsibility of each and every one of us.

Ethical decisions are at the root of all types of organisations and ethical issues have been reported regardless of organisational structure, industry and purpose. However, it seems that the NFP sector deserves a close look from an ethical point of view:

- *The purpose of the organisation is not always translated into ethical decisions and behaviours* – NFPs exist to serve the greater good, hence are commonly perceived by the public as ethical organisations. The media and public attention is typically focused on the ethics of for-profit organisations. However, many interviewees raised sincere concerns about unethical behaviours and board decisions in NFPs. One example is the practice of spending 75 per cent of fundraising on administration and salaries, while only 25 per cent is dedicated to the cause itself. Another common example was mismanagement of finances and reporting systems that wouldn't have been accepted by any for-profit standards.

- *Lack of structure and control processes* – while for-profit organisations operate under clear corporate governance and financial structures with control systems in place, in NFPs (especially small NFPs) these structures and control mechanisms often do not exist or are not well developed, providing fertile ground for unethical decisions and, in some cases, corruption. When ethical issues are raised, without a proper corporate governance system in place, they are more difficult to deal with. We would like to note that having a constitution in place does not equate to corporate governance, as the constitution still needs to be adhered to and the finance, corporate governance and control mechanisms should exist regardless of the organisational purpose – and this applies to both the for-profit and the not-for-profit sectors.

- *The delicate issue of volunteers* – many NFPs operate using volunteers throughout the organisation. With regard to volunteers who do the ground work, it is always a quandary how much structure and control can be exerted over people who volunteer and dedicate their time for the cause, many of whom take on tasks that not every employee would be happy to perform. It is the delicate balance between keeping volunteers happy and maintaining control over their work that is hard to achieve.

- *Board composition* – while management is typically paid, board members are volunteers. In many cases, people join NFP boards to gain experience, reputation, networking opportunities or for other personal reasons. Board positions in the NFP sector are typically unpaid and there is always a high need for directors in the sector. Consequently, some boards consist of a majority of inexperienced directors. Lack of experience coupled with a lack of robust systems of governance can place the organisation at significant ethical risk. Remember, most ethical problems in organisations are not the result of an intended criminal thought, but of lack of proper systems and attention to ethics.

The Johari Window

In 1955, two American psychologists, Joseph Luft and Harrington Ingham, devised a simple model to help people understand both themselves and others. They called this the Johari Window[14] and it focuses attention on what we know about ourselves or do not know about ourselves (one axis) and what others know about us or do not know about us (the second axis). Properly used, this tool enables a person to understand their 'arena' – that area which is known both to ourselves and to others; their 'façade' – that area which we know about ourselves but which is kept hidden from others; their 'blindspot' – that area which others know about us but of which we are unaware; and their 'unknown' – that area which is known neither to ourselves nor to others. This tool is now widely used in a variety of personal development processes but it has application also in the field of ethics and corporate behaviour – especially when we are considering the issue of personal ethics in relation to corporate ethics.

In all areas of life it is easy to see disconnects between what people espouse in public and what they do in their work situation. The higher a person's public profile, the easier it is to see such dissonance and, very often, it is these disconnects on which the media pounce when they have a point to make – politicians are a case in point, when a political party member is seen advocating and/or adhering to party policy even when this policy might be at odds with what they have previously stated or with the advocated practices of other groups to which they belong.

Company directors are not immune from these observations.

There are myriad examples of organisations acting in ways that are considered unethical. Over the years we have been regaled with accounts of how major companies such as Nike, Apple and other well-known brands across virtually every field of human endeavour work at maximising their profits by, in part, having their goods and/or services produced by workers in countries that are known to exploit the poor and disadvantaged. Many such examples are cited throughout this book and many more could be cited. Yet, when the directors of these companies are profiled it is clear that, in the main, they are men and women with impeccable credentials as highly ethical and moral people. So how does this disconnect arise? Why is it that one can get the impression that so many powerful, successful male and female professionals seem to have totally different personas depending on whether they are acting as a company director or as a general member of society at large?

The answer lies in the concept of the 'unknown'. The Johari Window makes it clear that the only way of reducing one's unknown is by both increasing the quantity and quality of what one reveals about oneself and, simultaneously, by accepting feedback from others on how you are perceived. Both of these are difficult to do – especially if self-revelation includes sharing one's real thoughts and emotions and if accepting feedback includes acceptance of comment which is extremely critical of one's behaviour. The more 'successful' one is perceived to be by one's peers and the more one feels the need to maintain an appropriate 'image' in society, the more difficult it becomes to accept both the self-revelation and the feedback process. Hans Christian Andersen's story of 'The Emperor's New Clothes' finds similarities every day in virtually every boardroom of every company across the world. People become so engrossed with their own role and so dismissive of 'lesser' beings that no one is really prepared to challenge behaviour. And, because there tend to be many overlapping boards among professional directors, the deception becomes self-perpetuating – surrounded by like-thinking people, nobody challenges the current orthodoxy.

Attempts to address this issue have increased since the 1980s, with a plethora of board assessment and board evaluation tools now available. However, few, if any, of these address the issue of personal values and personal ethics versus organisational values and organisational ethics. Instead, they tend to focus on the roles and responsibilities of directors and the extent to which each is suitably qualified for their role and sufficiently diligent in performing it. Ancient philosophers such as Plato, Aeschylus and Socrates all argued that one of the most important challenges for a person is to 'know thyself'. We suggest this is equally important for an organisation. Paying attention to the Johari Window process from an organisational perspective can help directors do just that. When that happens, we should be able to discern a reduction in the frequency and size of gaps between what is personally espoused and what is actually done in and by corporations.

Emotional intelligence

In 1995, Daniel Goleman introduced a concept he called 'emotional intelligence'.[15] Goleman argued that, while traditional leadership qualities such as intelligence, toughness, determination and vision are required for success, they are inadequate on their own. His research found that those organisations which are optimally successful have leaders that are really effective because they have the additional qualities of self-awareness, self-regulation, motivation, empathy and social skills. He demonstrated that there was a direct, positive correlation between these 'soft' skills and measurable business results.

Later research (in the early twenty-first century) by John Angelidis and Nabil A. Ibrahim[16] extended this investigation to look at the relationship between emotional intelligence and business ethics. They found that managers who exhibit higher emotional intelligence believe that actions should neither be deceptive nor harm others. Those managers who exhibit lower emotional intelligence, however, are willing to take actions that have negative consequences for others. In other words, Angelidis and Ibrahim's study demonstrated that the level of emotional intelligence is strongly correlated with ethical behaviour.

There is a further correlation here with the Johari Window concept. Emotional intelligence can be summarised as having four key components:

1 Self-awareness in terms of my values and beliefs and how I come across to others – my operating style.
2 Awareness of others in terms of their values and beliefs and how they come across to others – their operating styles.
3 The extent to which I demonstrate the ability to flex my operating style so that it improves my communication with others.
4 The extent to which I exhibit self-control when experiencing stress, no matter how it is caused or where it is encountered.

It is easy to see that this relates extremely closely to the Johari Window concept of enlarging one's arena through self-disclosure and acceptance of feedback. If I am aware of how I come across to others and demonstrate high levels of flexibility in relating to the way other people think and act then I will be perceived as a person who can be trusted to do the right thing – even when 'the right thing' is different from what my peers and 'the establishment' believe is 'doing things right'. As Angelidis and Ibrahim argue, I will tend to act ethically rather than unethically.

This, of course, is particularly pertinent for company directors. As has already been stated, the board ultimately determines an organisation's culture. What the chair and other directors are heard to say and what they are seen to do is constantly evaluated by everyone outside the board. If there is inconsistency between words and actions, if there are verbal gymnastics to justify limitations on what is said or done, if there are huge gaps between what is done for people at the top of an organisation and what is done for those at the bottom of the organisation and/or for its customers, then a broad perception of the organisation being unethical is likely to develop.

Notes

1 Fletcher, J. (1997) *Situation Ethics: The New Morality*, Westminster John Knox Press, Louisville, Kentucky, USA.
2 Fletcher's earlier book, *Situation Ethics*, was published in 1966.
3 Beck, D. and Cowan, C. (1996) *Spiral Dynamics: Mastering Values, Leadership and Change*, Blackwell, USA.
4 Covey, S. R. (1991) *Principle Centred Leadership*, Fireside, New York.
5 *Sydney Morning Herald*, 30 April 2015.
6 All figures are given in Australian dollars unless otherwise stated.
7 Information about this is available from most Australian media archives as well as from the Australian Securities and Investment Commission (ASIC) records.
8 See http://www.abc.net.au/news/2015-05-04/supermarkets-food-outlets-exploit-black-market-migrant-workers/6441496 [20 July 2016].
9 Anderson, R. and White, R. (2011) *The Power of One Good Question: Confessions of a Radical Industrialist*, Random House Business Books, London, UK.
10 See http://www.theage.com.au/victoria/health-experts-warn-against-fast-food-at-monash-childrens-hospital-20141228-12c9et.html [20 July 2016].
11 Hand, G. (2001) *Naked Among Cannibals*, Allen & Unwin, Crows Nest, Australia.
12 Available at http://www.canberratimes.com.au/business/banking-and-finance/banking-on-ethics-is-risky-business-20151223-gltz35.html [20 July 2016].
13 'Sustainable tea at Unilever', Harvard Business School, 21 December 2011.
14 Luft, J. and Ingham, H. (1955) The Johari Window: A graphic model of interpersonal awareness, *Proceedings of the Western Training Laboratory in Group Development*, Los Angeles, University of California.
15 Goleman, D. (1995) *Emotional Intelligence*, Bantam Dell Publishing Group, New York.
16 Angelidis, J. and Ibrahim, N. A. (2011) The impact of emotional intelligence on the ethical judgement of managers, *Journal of Business Ethics*, Vol. 99, pp. 111–119.

3 Organisational culture

The complex issue of culture

Some years ago, the then chairman of a major international airline met with Doug to discuss issues that had arisen among flight crew. Like all airlines, this one had as its primary concern the issue of passenger safety. However, growth had meant that they needed to recruit flight crew from other countries and, at times, this had resulted in significant conflict on the flight deck with overseas trained personnel being reluctant to accept nationally trained people in positions of authority. In understanding the reason for this, and also in order to find a way forward, Doug referred to the studies of Geert Hofstede,[1] which provided some insight into the cultural norms of different societies. Using these insights it became possible to develop understanding and to promote functional rather than dysfunctional conflict on the flight deck.

As already indicated in the previous chapter, different societies (and often different groups in the same society) can have different standards in relation to a wide range of matters. These different standards reflect different cultures and they are seen in the skills, arts, beliefs, customs and behaviours that have been (and are) passed from one generation to the next.

For many years, cultural differences among groups of people were observed, sometimes tolerated and, if you were from the dominant grouping, seen as something to be eradicated. So it was in foreign countries controlled by powers like Great Britain, France, Germany, Belgium, Portugal, Spain, China, Japan and in their own countries, such as Australia and the United States (among others), that indigenous people (at least in their own country) were either seen as 'sub-human' or as 'primitive' beings who needed to be controlled and developed so that, perhaps, they could be assimilated into 'civilised' society. (Even today, in 2016, some ethnic groups experience resistance to their migration into developed countries because they are perceived (usually quite erroneously) as being unable to conform to the norms of their new society.) Then, in 1991, Hofstede published a book[2] that reported on research he had done both with IBM during the years around 1970 and additional independent research. In this (and also in his other writings) he argued that national characteristics – culture – could be identified and classified by considering five dimensions: individualistic vs collectivistic, high power distance vs low power distance, high certainty avoidance vs low certainty avoidance, achievement vs nurturing and long-term orientation vs short-term orientation. He went on to show groupings of similar nations/peoples using these criteria.[3]

While there are many criticisms of Hofstede's work and some people believe much of his research was flawed, the fact remains that he gave us a framework by which to understand why different groupings of people act in different ways. He gave us a framework by which culture can be assessed and understood. This understanding can help us relate better both to those who are in similar groupings and to those in totally different groupings. With this tool we no longer need to concentrate on the differences between us but, by understanding the 'what, why and how' of any differences, use this knowledge to concentrate on what we have in common and so move forward together in a positive manner.

During the 1990s and early 2000s, a team lead by Professor Michael House[4] of Wharton Business School, University of Pennsylvania, revisited Hofstede's work and studied 62 countries across ten global clusters. The study, known as the GLOBE (Global Leadership and Organizational Behavior Effectiveness) Project, ascertained nine cultural characteristics (or 'cultural competencies') that echoed Hofstede's original characteristics while also refining and adding to these. The GLOBE Project again made very clear the importance of understanding and working with cultural differences to achieve a successful outcome. It also highlighted the difficulties that arise when one seeks to change these ingrained cultures.

By definition, culture is neutral – it is only when we consider it in relation to some particular context that value judgements can be made. 'Culture' is simply a short-hand expression to describe the skills, arts, beliefs, customs and behaviours that are passed from one generation to the next, whether at a national, organisational or family level. It is therefore vital that when a board is considering its future it assesses the existing organisational culture in relation to the desired future organisation so that clashes between strategy and culture can be identified and addressed.

Over time, it has become clear that real cultural change requires an evolutionary rather than a revolutionary process. While revolutionary and enforced change might bring about instrumental compliance with the wishes of the change initiators and the powerful, when 'the tumult and the shouting dies, the captains and the kings depart',[5] and the suppressed culture rapidly re-emerges because, at the core, it never went away. We see this time and time again in both the public and private sectors. Far too often, there is outward compliance with the dictates from the top but, deep down, there is a subtle erosion at work – akin to the covert action of termites undermining the fundamental integrity of a structure – which reduces the overall success level of the change initiative, and management is largely powerless to address this unless they have a very deep understanding of the real culture that is driving organisational performance and are prepared to commit to the time and cost necessary. Real culture change is not a short-term project and should not be addressed by a 'quick fix' approach which focuses on the surface issues without addressing the hidden underpinnings that ultimately drive behaviour.

It is here that Hofstede's work and the GLOBE Project can be most valuable. Using these frameworks, the culture of an organisation or of a sub-group within an organisation can be mapped, its relative strengths and weaknesses ascertained and a plan developed to facilitate whatever change may be deemed necessary – preferably in some form of fast-tracked evolutionary process. Culture can change but it takes considerable time and it is not an easy process.

Culture has an extremely significant impact on whether or not any organisation achieves its desired objectives. Within an organisation (public or private sector), though, it is a combination of cultures that become important. There is plenty of evidence to show that an organisation's strategy needs to be supported (or at the very least not opposed either covertly or overtly) if the strategy is going to have a reasonable chance of successful implementation. Many studies have been carried out which indicate that somewhere around 80 per cent of all change initiatives fail to achieve their full desired benefits – and successful strategy implementation invariably requires some changes – with the cause being traced back to cultural issues.

One of the most important works relating to this issue is Kotter and Heskett's *Corporate Culture and Performance*,[6] published in 1992. From their study of 22 businesses, they concluded that effective strategy implementation requires an internal 'adaptive' culture. In other words, throughout the organisation, there needs to be consistent behaviour that clearly demonstrates a deep, practical concern for customers, stockholders and employees. Part of this concern is the need to operate ethically as well as in accordance with the law.

There are, however, also issues of national culture that impact on successful strategy implementation. For example, a strategy to increase an organisation's profitability through sales of pork and related products in either Israel or any Muslim countries, or through significant alcoholic beverage sales in most Muslim countries is obviously extremely unlikely to be successful because of national religious and cultural issues.

Although ethical systems do not have national boundaries, the notion and elements of ethics differ, sometimes even contradict, between countries. A common practice in one culture can be perceived as unethical and even illegal in a different country. As globalisation becomes the obvious reality, boards are now facing new ethical challenges.

About ten years ago, during her PhD research, Zivit went to interview human resources (HR) people in a Chinese subsidiary of a global company. Surprisingly, both HR interviewees were in tears about the huge loss of face with which they were dealing. As loyal employees, they worked very hard to get *Guanxi* (connection) with a certain bureaucrat and tailored a position to suit his cousin. In return, they received tax deductions for the company and its Chinese employees. This was perceived as a great achievement within the Chinese subsidiary. However, during the regular yearly global process, the auditors realised that, with the same unit sales in China, the revenues were now significantly higher. When the company's headquarters found out what had happened, they immediately ordered the subsidiary to pay the entire regular tax, saying that they cannot report revenues using unethical practices. Employees had to start paying the normal level of tax as well. The HR team, who, as loyal employees had extensively used their own *Guanxi* for the benefit of the company, lost face. In their words:

Interviewee 1:   You know, we have the rule here and the people should follow the rule, and maybe you can go this way to reach the rule, or maybe go this way [shows different indirect ways with her hands]. But maybe for the foreigner they just go this way [shows a straight line with her hand].

Interviewee 2:   Some local companies are operating in a grey area.

Interviewee 1:   I say, most of the majority of local companies are operating like this way. An example is the tax issue. Because in here there is a room, you can move forward to save a lot of money.

Interviewee 2:   Our taxes follow the national policy. But maybe we can use the other rule to decrease the tax. The company says we should follow this rule, so we cannot have that.

Interviewee 1:   It doesn't mean we follow; just the corporate is very stiff. Sometimes we have some kind of the right way, we can try to reduce – but they don't want to try it. Because, as I understand, we are a multinational company, we are a stock exchange listed company, we should comply with everything. They don't take the risk.

Interviewee 2:   But this is not a risk [laughs].

Interviewee 1:   I say, *it's not a risk!* Because in here, as I told you, the majority of companies, they do it this way. And also a lot of things I like to tell you – in China they are very contractive with Guanxi, which means relationships. In the US company they don't think so, they just say: 'everything just follows compliance'. *The regulations! Guanxi is related to everything!*

Interviewee 2:   Like you have relationships with the tax bureaucrat or other legal bureaucrat, so you will have a ...

Interviewee 1:   They will have you, or maybe they can teach you how to reduce the tax. They will teach you ... *Still it is legal!* They will teach you the legal way to reduce or avoid some taxes.

Concepts like *Guanxi* are ethical principles. Cause and effect are strongly connected to this concept. In their culture, the use of *Guanxi* was both ethical and good business practice. In their quest to do what was best for their employer it was an appropriate lever to utilise in order to achieve desired results. However, in a totally different culture and from the perspective of auditors who were entrenched in this 'outside' culture, the effect of improved returns arose through the use of an inappropriate cause. The auditors' consideration of cause and effect led to a determination that the end did not justify the means – and this determination led to serious personal cost for people who, through ignorance of the different standards being applied to their operations on a universal basis, had operated in a way they thought was appropriate. A proactive approach by the parent company in which every employee throughout their empire was fully educated in relation to what was or was not considered 'ethical behaviour' might have avoided much embarrassment for all the parties involved.

Another example of ethics differing among cultures was provided by a chairperson of a global company. 'We wanted to bid for a project in the Philippines ... needed to bribe and hence decided not to bid. We didn't want to have to operate unethically.' Operating according to the ethical system and legal environment of the headquarters meant losing a business opportunity.

Today's global business arena means that it is no longer sufficient to solve a problem from the point of view of just one mindset. We need to be cross-cultural and share interpretations of world views. The concept of right and wrong differs between cultures and, in order to work together, we may need to see things from a different perspective.

There is absolutely no doubt that boards need to have clear rules of what is proper and what is not and they need to apply the rules globally. But simply issuing a blanket 'motherhood' statement, which though reassuring fails to resolve the issue, in relation to values or 'guiding principles' is not enough. As indicated by Zivit's example, clear communication of desired behaviours is also necessary if boards are going to be able to deal with different types of governance issues in each culture.

David Martin[7] argues that, across almost all of the developed and developing world, life is aligned with a domination and control approach that relies heavily on Adam Smith's 1776 opus *The Wealth of Nations*,[8] in which all aspects of nature – including human beings – are 'resources' over which structures of power must exert dominion; an integral trade framework. The result is, Martin says, that:

> Rather than bathing in the cosmic ocean of abundance, we have built systems that manage scarcity (time, resources, order, control, and money) while allowing our power to be transferred to surrogates who construct and maintain their position by the manufacture and perpetuation of fear.

Martin goes on to argue that we need a system that can unleash our unfettered humanity in persistent, generative action. He proposes an approach that recognises the reality of resources' abundance, available in every organisation, and then empowers people to release the innovation and creativity they contain. The movement is away from fear towards trust and the development of individual and organisational accountability and responsibility. Martin describes an audit process in which organisations consider the quantity (whether positives or negatives) of commodities, culture and custom, knowledge, money, technology and well-being currently available to them, assess each of these in terms of the positive or negative impact they have and then examine how these can be harnessed by empowering people to achieve results.

The beauty of this approach is that it provides a creative and innovative means for assessing existing organisational culture while, simultaneously, providing indicators of possible beneficial culture shifts available. By including such areas as culture and custom, knowledge and well-being this approach also ensures that the issue of ethics is confronted by the enforced requirement to consider far wider perspectives than those with a primarily economic focus. Accordingly, such an audit can facilitate a move towards ethical operations.

But what does all this talk about 'culture' have to do with the issue of corporate governance and ethical behaviour?

Anthropologists have shown that virtually all societies and cultures develop basic codes of conduct that include ethical standards. Read any of the holy books from the world's religions and they all contain information on how people should behave and treat each other. There is a combination of both 'law' and 'ethics'. Of course, looking at how adherents to any of those faiths actually behave shows that many day-to-day behaviours fall short of the ideals set out in the Torah, the Koran, the Bible, the Upanishads, etc., but the point is that, by reference back to the core of one's faith it becomes possible to ascertain what one ought to do and, if one is really serious about one's faith, to make appropriate behavioural changes.

And this is why a discussion of culture is both important and has relevance to corporate governance. If we want people throughout any organisation to know how they ought to behave, then we need to precisely clarify the behavioural standards that ought to be followed. This is a central responsibility of the board. It then follows that a subsidiary responsibility of the board is to create the organisational environment in which people at all levels know the desired standards, see the desired standards demonstrated by those at the very highest organisational levels and, over time, become committed themselves to observing these standards in their own behaviour. In other words, the board defines and models the desired organisational culture while putting in place rewards and sanctions that will enhance the probability of the desired behaviours becoming an everyday reality across the organisation, no matter where in the world it may be operating.

So let us now consider the matter of organisational culture

Culture: achiever or deceiver?

The issue of culture from the perspective of a board's ethical responsibilities is extremely complex. As we have stated above, the culture of an organisation ultimately reflects the real values that drive an organisation's performance. Organisational culture, in general terms, refers to 'the way we do things around here'. The primary responsibility for determining, promulgating and modelling this culture lies with the board and, pre-eminently, with the chair.

Chairs we interviewed made comments such as:

> If you get your culture right, you will succeed!
> Culture does matter.

Whether or not this is widely acknowledged, the fact is that ethics (or a lack thereof) is part of the organisational culture. However, culture, despite being widely analysed and discussed in business publications and management education for decades, somehow still appears to be a new area for a number of boards. Many directors state that they are finding it hard to measure, lead or govern culture. A possible reason for this is that culture is a soft concept about which most board members have not been trained or which, when they did encounter it as part of their formal studies, was perceived as being largely irrelevant or subsidiary to the more important subjects that related to law, accounting, finance and other 'hard' concepts. Today, there needs to be a clear understanding that culture is not about writing a report or reading a document. Culture is the actual lifeblood of the organisation. As one chairman said:

> It is an ongoing commitment and obligation of the organisation. It's part of the organisational DNA.

Deep down, many boards and organisations do appreciate this – even if they fail to comprehend how to deal with it. Although they may not fully understand it, the issue of managing the culture to get a better ethical outcome was a common topic raised by many interviewees. As one chairman said:

> How can I make the corporate to be ethically sound? How can I make the culture to be more productive and profitable? More efficient, better run, better structured …

In the previous chapter we discussed how culture evolves through the skills, arts, beliefs, customs and behaviours that are passed from one generation to the next. The same is true of organisations. If, in the early days of an organisation's existence, inappropriate behaviour is, at best, tolerated or, at worst, actively rewarded, promoted or otherwise encouraged then, over time, that inappropriate behaviour will become 'the way we do things around here' – the 'norm' – for that organisation. Both Trevor Sykes and Andrew Main, whose works were referred to in Chapter 1, show very clearly how the cultures that led to the demise of a significant number of Australian organisations during the 1990s developed from blatantly inappropriate behaviours being either ignored or actively condoned and encouraged from a very early stage.

Culture from the top: the role of boards in organisational culture

As one chairman put it:

> Culture, culture, culture! What do we actually allow, accept and expect …

Here is an interesting dilemma which every board member faces. On the one hand, board members are personally liable for what is going on in the organisation, including its culture and ethics. On the other hand, both culture and ethics are intangible concepts – hard to measure, hard to report on, hard to capture, especially when boards are meeting once a month and the organisation is large, complex and geographically dispersed.

Poor organisational culture has been identified as the underlying cause of ethical issues and corporate misconduct. An analysis of the global financial crisis concluded that it was caused by systemic ethical issues.[9] At the individual level, poor cultures create a lack of trust and an environment where people cannot perform to their best abilities. Good culture is associated with organisational success. Hence, creating a good corporate culture by setting the tone from the top should be one of the board's top priorities.

This is an area where many boards need to develop. Board members traditionally come from 'hard' disciplines, such as law and accounting, and hence directors may be less aware of and less experienced in working with culture, cultural change management and leadership of ethics. Any fear of these 'fluffy' concepts is unjustified. At the end of the day, it means to consciously lead, govern and run the business according to your own attitude and values, your personal ethical system.

The Ethics Resource Centre in the United States[10] reports that the National Business Ethics Survey conducted in 2016 in large organisations found that, in organisations that do not have an effective ethics programme, 62 per cent of employees have observed misconduct but only 32 per cent of these reported to their management or other authorities that they had observed wrongdoing. In organisations that have an effective programme in place, 33 per cent of employees observed misconduct and 87 per cent of these reported their observation. In those organisations that do not manage ethics effectively, 59 per cent of the employees that reported the misconduct experienced retaliation, in comparison with 4 per cent in organisations that have ethical programmes in place. Any form of retaliation (overt or covert) is a clear cultural tool that conveys the message not to report observations of ethical issues and misconduct. Another finding is that in those organisations that do not have an ethics programme in place, 23 per cent of employees reported pressure to compromise on standards. In contrast, only 3 per cent of employees in organisations that have an ethics programme reported the same pressure. These findings are a call for action for all boards, regardless of the organisation's size or purpose. The survey reveals the significant number of ethical issues that organisations are facing, while at the same time illustrating that explicitly managing ethics in organisations is not only possible, but also yields good results.

In terms of directorship, it means having explicit discussions in the boardroom about culture and ethics, setting guidelines and modelling the right behaviours. The issue of ethics should be an essential item on the agenda at every board meeting. The governance role here is built on receiving reports from the executives about the culture and its ethical processes. But waiting for such reports from executives, while at least a step in the right direction, is not enough. Board members should not simply rely on these reports, but should visit all areas of the organisation and speak with its employees, suppliers, partners and customers in order to get a clearer picture of the actual organisational culture and its ethical operations. As one local chair of a very large and very well-respected public multinational company stated, 'a critical part of my role is visiting our clients and suppliers to discuss any issues and/or concerns about any of our behaviours by any person and in any place'.

The importance of directors moving around their organisation and being aware of the culture was highlighted by Greg Medcraft, chair of the Australian Securities and Investment Commission (ASIC) when, on 21 June 2016 he was reported as saying that:[11]

> while ... monitoring culture by those directors not involved in the daily operations was 'a challenge' he urged boards to ensure the culture of the organisation was being independently assessed and whether the stated culture was consistent with the experiences of customers, employees and suppliers.

Medcraft went on to say:

> In terms of what ASIC will do, where we identify poor culture, we will make this clear to the firms in which we see it. It is important to share this information with directors given their role in guiding and monitoring the management of the company.

Despite the opposition from many directors (as also reported in the same article) there can little doubt that, at least in Australia, this awareness and monitoring of culture will become an increasingly important area in which directors must become involved.

Modelling culture

While everyone acknowledges that all boards have a duty of care, in many companies the full complexity of that duty of care seems to get lost. As one chairman said:

> We still have a legacy of command and control that leads to bullying. At director level – monkeys see, monkeys do. It starts with the leadership and becomes systemic.

Some companies are 'rotten from the head'. Chairpersons and board members need to 'walk the talk' in order to implement an ethical culture. When there is bullying and humiliation in the boardroom, you cannot expect the organisational culture to have high ethical standards. Culture is defined by the behaviours of the leaders, not by what they say.

One chair told the following story:

> A friend of mine was a chair of [a major sporting] club. He had parties with cocaine in his house – if you believe what people say about him. The story is that he then lent money to the CEO, who was addicted to gambling (which the chairperson was aware of) …

The personal modelling approach is the best advice here – always act in an ethical and lawful manner with your employees.

> I have very high ethical standards and never allow myself to compromise.

On 18 March 2015, the *Australian Financial Review* carried an article about the demise of Orica's CEO[12] because of his behaviour, despite the good financial results. He was doing what the company expected in terms of organisational performance but his personal behaviour was considered to be overly aggressive. This is an example of a board that cares about ethics and culture.

In contrast, there are many examples of HR professionals who found themselves on the wrong side of the ethical debate and lost their job by fighting for the right decision. Cases related to mergers and acquisitions, payment of employees' entitlements, transparency of head-count reporting to the board and other examples where HR managers, in their efforts to ensure that the organisation is doing the right thing, have lost their job while championing corporate ethics. A well-accepted practice is that when the chief financial officer (CFO) resigns, a board member conducts the exit interview. However, when the chief of culture (and hence ethics) leaves the company, not many boards pay attention and ask why. And so, the team that can help the board in unlocking the true organisational culture and ethical systems, which leads decisions on the floor (rather than on the policy paper), is overlooked. It is not surprising then that cases like Volkswagen (VW) 'pop up out of the blue'.

The 2015 case of VW

Relatively recently, the world was astonished by the fraud perpetrated by VW, which involved adding software to 11 million diesel cars in order to have them meet the emission standards on the test stand, but not in reality on the road. Whether the board knew about it or not will probably be investigated. But the one fact we are in no doubt about is that this sham, occurring for so long without being detected, means that the organisational culture was tolerant, and even supportive, of unethical decision making and behaviours. It could have been prevented if the organisational culture had been based on clear ethical boundaries.

This software was a collaboration which required involvement from the lowest technician to the highest executive. There were people who were involved in covering up the fraud and duping the regulators who were trying to uncover why the emissions differed between results on the test stand and the actual pollution recorded when driving on the highway. Even if only a few people knew about it, the need to develop such a software indicates a true organisational problem. It implies that VW did not have an effective ethical framework to guide decisions and behaviours.

We would like to emphasise the word 'effective', since VW does have an ethics statement on its company website:[13]

> The Volkswagen Group has always considered itself bound by more than just legal and internal regulations. We also see voluntary commitments and ethical principles as an integral component of our corporate culture, providing a frame of reference we can use to guide our decision-making.

In considering this example, it is important to look at what VW (on other company websites) itself says about ethics. On the web, Volkswagen Italy's public statement that introduces the 18-page statement on the Organization, Management, and Control Model[14] says:

Dear colleagues,

Since its foundation, VOLKSWAGEN GROUP ITALIA S.P.A. has believed that ethical conduct is a basic principle to reaching its company objectives.

The Code of Ethics presented to you is proof of daily operations marked by the principles of honesty, fairness, and respect which are the guiding values of the people who work with VOLKSWAGEN GROUP ITALIA S.P.A..

The Code of Ethics also represents a guarantee for all internal and external stakeholders of the Company that their individual and professional rights will be consistently assured.

It is our pleasure to share with you the Code of Ethics of the VOLKSWAGEN GROUP ITALIA S.P.A., as an essential reference model for conduct, which identifies the values we believe in as individuals and as a company.

M. Nordio M. Obrowsk

The same introductory page goes on to assure readers that:

The Code is an essential part of the Organization, Management and Control Model required by article 6 of the Legislative Decree 231/01 bearing the 'Regulations on the administrative responsibility of legal persons and of bodies without legal personality, pursuant to article 11 of Italian Law 300 of 29 September 2000'.

Given the ethical issues currently being faced by the company, Volkswagen's statement on the environment from the same document is especially interesting. It states:

2.7 Environmental protection

In order to carry out an eco-friendly and socially sustainable mobility, the Volkswagen Group is committed to producing and distributing its automobiles with the lowest environmental impact and to investing in the development of ecologically efficient advanced technologies.

VOLKSWAGEN GROUP ITALIA S.P.A. aims to increase the use of alternative power sources in order to satisfy its energetic demand and promotes such eco-friendly behaviours also among its dealers and service partners.

The Company is committed to encouraging each employee to make appropriate and economical use of natural resources and ensure that its activities have the lowest influence on the environment.

The document also sets out specific guidelines for managers:

3.5.4 Management

Each manager serves as a role model and must act in strict accordance with the Code of Ethics, and has the duty to promote and spread its values and principles among his or her employees.

Each manager has responsibility for his or her employees. The relationship must be based on mutual respect.

Managers must provide support and adequate information, agree with employees upon clear, ambitious and realistic goals and promote the job development of their employees.

As one reads the pages of this document it is clear that, if the ethical framework outlined in the document were really being implemented then there is no way that this scandal could ever have eventuated. Clearly, a gap existed (and perhaps still exists) between what is written (i.e. publically espoused) and what is done. The basis for an ethical framework of behaviour is obvious: the actualisation of an ethical behaviour is less clear. (As an aside, it must be noted that since the VW saga emerged it has become clear that the practice of manipulating emissions data is not confined to VW but rather appears to be quite widespread across the industry.)

So, an ethics statement on its own is not enough. The practice of appropriate ethical standards needs to be truly embedded in the company culture, otherwise leaders and employees might breach it. If the culture is not supportive of ethics, then no statement will work.

When leaders decide to ignore a code of ethics, they are driven by certain motivators. What positive outcomes did they think they would get in return? Did they feel that it was safe to breach the code? Or maybe there was group thinking at work – something that can occur when leaders recruit and retain only those who think like they do and tell them what they want to hear? All these questions, and many others, point to the same direction: corporate culture.

This is a great challenge for board members, especially for those who are used to governing by focusing their attention on 'hard' information, such as policies, and are relatively detached from the company's day-to-day reality. How are they supposed to know what is really going on at grassroots level? What is the true (rather than stated) culture of the organisation? The example from VW is a case that emphasises how necessary it is for the board to actively direct and govern ethics rather than passively assuming that a clear ethics statement will suffice to ensure appropriate behaviour.

The competencies for changing culture

Some years ago, research by two Australian researchers, Dennis Turner and Michael Crawford, indicated that there were 16 competencies that drive corporate renewal.[15] While these competencies consider the renewal of an organisation overall and, as such, they all have relevance for changing an organisation's culture, the competencies of performance control, motivating and enthusing, integration, enaction, communication and achieving commitment are particularly pertinent to culture change.

Turner and Crawford provide the following descriptions of these competencies:

- Performance control is setting goals, monitoring what happens and taking action to keep performance on target.
- Motivating and enthusing is getting people motivated about their work and the firm.
- Integration is achieving coordinated action throughout the firm.
- Enaction is taking timely and effective action, not just planning and talking about things.
- Communication throughout the firm is communicating on matters relevant to people and their work.
- Achieving commitment is achieving widespread commitment to carrying out decisions.

As already stated, Turner and Crawford apply these (and the rest of the 16 competencies) to the renewal of an organisation overall, but they have a direct relationship to ensuring that the ethical stand promulgated in an organisation's corporate documentation is actually enacted throughout the organisation. As examples such as the VW scandal make clear, it is not enough for a board and/or executive team to develop a values statement and a code of ethics that can be displayed on the company's website and in all formal documents. For an organisation to be widely seen as ethical there must be consistent behaviour at every organisational level and across every organisational area – and that starts by the board and executive team first being totally consistent in word and action and then monitoring this throughout the organisation. But you cannot do this by sitting in an office and waiting for exception reports to meander their way up the organisational chain – you need to be seen to be out there and to be taking remedial action as soon as inappropriate behaviour is observed or otherwise discovered. This is a key role, not only for managers and executives, but also (and very importantly) for the board and chair. If it is true that people concentrate on those things to which 'the boss pays attention' then, in an issue such as ethics, it is imperative that the most senior bosses of all – the chair and directors – are seen as actively ensuring that the right behaviour is adhered to. The actions of a board in concentrating on these competencies identified by Turner and Crawford can go an extremely long way towards bringing about an ethical culture of which every stakeholder can be proud.

What do you do when your competitors gain advantage through unethical practices?

In December 2015, the *Sydney Morning Herald* carried a story about alleged unconscionable (i.e. unethical) conduct by one of Australia's major retail chains.[16] (This case came to court early in 2016 and, at the time of publication, is still before the courts.) It is alleged that Woolworths placed pressure on suppliers to pay a levy in order to reduce its half-yearly profit shortfall. Legal action was instituted by the Australian Competition and Consumer Commission (ACCC) and ACCC's chairman made the point that this alleged action by Woolworths was 'extremely egregious' given that, at the same time, the ACCC 'were in court in relation to Coles [Woolworths' major competitor] and our [ACCC's] proven unconscionable behaviour to their suppliers and that was all over the newspapers'. The report makes the point that, in December 2014, at the same time that Woolworths' senior management approved the $60 million 'Mind the Gap' scheme, Coles was fined $10 million in the Federal Court over unconscionable conduct in its dealings with suppliers in 2011.

So what are the limits within which an organisation has to work when seeking to compete?

The very first consideration is that competition must comply with the law. From the ACCC's perspective it would appear that neither retail chain was doing this – hence the legal action. But, as we have been arguing throughout this book, any action must not only be legal, it should also be ethical. If the test of 'ethical' concerns the minimum consideration of public perception – how would you feel if this action was splashed across the front pages of major daily newspapers – then this alone should have been sufficient for both retail chains to have taken quite different actions. The fact that it at least pushed, and possibly also broke, the legal boundaries simply makes more obvious the shortcomings of corporate governance.

At some time or another almost every organisation is confronted by competitors that seem to be using an 'end justifies the means' approach to gaining market share and improving profits. This presents a further challenge for boards to confront. Did the management of Woolworths, in the example above, believe that Coles' behaviour was disadvantaging them and so decide that an 'if you can't beat them, then join them' approach was justified? Which of the two organisations was actually the first to start at least considering (if not implementing) inappropriate behaviours? We shall probably never know the answer to those questions, but we do know that the end result for both organisations was expensive. It takes strong management, supported by a highly ethical board, to maintain high standards of behaviour when the competition is using questionable tactics. And it takes a board in which each director is actively out visiting and observing what is taking place at every level and in every part of the organisation to maximise the probability that inappropriate behaviours will be recognised and stopped at their inception.

Notes

1 Hofstede, G. (1984) *Culture's Consequences: International Differences in Work-Related Values* (2nd edn), Beverly Hills, CA, Sage Publications.
2 Hofstede, G., Hofstede, G. J. and Minkov, M. (1991) *Cultures and Organizations: Software of the Mind*, New York, McGraw-Hill.
3 For more recent information on Hofstede's concepts, refer to Hofstede, G. J., Hofstede, G. J. and Minkov, M. (2005) *Cultures and Organizations: Software of the Mind* (revised and expanded 2nd edn), New York, McGraw-Hill.
4 House, R. J., Hanges, P. J., Javidan, M., Dorfman, P. W. and Gupta, V. (eds) (2004) *Culture, Leadership, and Organizations: The GLOBE Study of 62 Societies*, Thousand Oaks, CA, Sage Publications.
5 Kipling, R. (1897) 'Recessional'.
6 Kotter, J. P. and Heskett, J. L. (1992) *Corporate Culture and Performance*, The Free Press, New York.
7 Martin, D. (2014) An inquiry into human nature and the cost of the wealth of nations: Addressing global systems failure through an integral systems paradigm for sustainable development, *AI & Society*, Vol. 29, Issue 2, May, pp. 143–148.
8 Smith, A. (1981[1776]) *The Wealth of Nations*, A. Skinner (ed.) reproduced by Penguin Books, Harmondsworth, UK.
9 See https://www.businessthink.unsw.edu.au/Pages/Post-Crisis-Ethics-Shifting-Mindsets-or-Business-as-Usual.aspx [21 July 2016].
10 See https://www.ethics.org/home [21 July 2016].
11 Available at http://www.smh.com.au/business/workplace-relations/asic-says-hand soff-company-directors-must-get-their-noses-in-to-culture-20160621-gpofey.html [21 July 2016].
12 See http://www.afr.com/brand/chanticleer/demise-of-orica-chief-ian-smith-a-lesson-for-boards-20150317-1m1pg2 [21 July 2016].
13 Available at www.volkswagenag.com/content/vwcorp/content/en/the_group/compliance.bin.html/pdfFile/compliance.pdf [21 July 2016].
14 Available at http://www.volkswagengroup.it/Apps/WebObjects/VGI.woa/1/wa/viewFile?id=260&lang=eng [21 July 2016].
15 Turner, D. and Crawford, M. (1998) *Change Power: Capabilities That Drive Corporate Renewal*, Business & Professional Publishing, Warriewood, NSW, Australia.
16 Available at http://www.smh.com.au/business/retail/accc-accuses-woolworths-of-unconscionable-conduct-20151210-glkfz2.html [21 July 2016].

4 Leadership

So far we have implied, but not specifically addressed, the issue of leadership. In many ways, this is 'the elephant in the room'.

As a general rule, boards are comprised of men and women who either are currently, or who have a record of being, successful in their chosen careers. Some have achieved this in their professional field of accounting, law, engineering and the like, while others have achieved success through their journey up organisational ladders. By definition, these people are used to having power and to exercising their authority. They are, in the main, respected by both their peers and the community in general. In some instances they have previously been the CEO of the organisation of which they are now a director. Yet, because only one of their number can be the chair, this can create the temptation for at least some of the directors to focus more on their area of speciality and how this impacts on organisational performance rather than implementing their more comprehensive role in relation to the governance of the organisation overall.

A major researcher, Elliott Jaques, made the point some years ago that leadership is not a generic concept. He argued that you can only really understand and/or develop leadership when you recognise the context within which leadership is being provided.[1] His point is that effective leadership is always dependent upon a range of factors and the way in which it is exercised can vary significantly across the levels, areas and types of organisations in which people live and work. His studies make it clear that there is a critical need for people at executive and board level of any organisation to have the conceptual ability to understand and deal with levels of ambiguity and complexity across a future well in excess of ten years, even if they know that their 'watch' will end long before that. This was reflected in a report featured in the *Sydney Morning Herald* of 3 June 2016, when an earlier Executive Chairman of Woolworths Ltd (Paul Simons, who transformed the company in the early 1990s) was reported by journalist Michael Pascoe[2] as attributing the blame for the current problems at Woolworths (one of Australia's major retail chains) to two men who ran the company in the early 2000s and who seemed to have moved the emphasis away from a focus on the customer and long-term wealth creation to a focus on maximising relatively short-term revenues and profits with the result that an 'end justifies the means' culture may have developed and may be the cause of the company's current situation.

Organisations with excellent corporate governance consider Jaques' work carefully and make sure it is recognised and applied. Accordingly, they ensure that people at different levels are able to fulfil leadership roles appropriate for their position.

As Doug has said elsewhere,[3] it is only in relatively recent years that leadership has become a serious subject in its own right.[4] Although leadership has been practised and discussed for countless years, most modern interpretations had their genesis in studies that commenced around 1939. Probably the best known of these early studies are those of the late 1940s at Ohio State University, which were able to provide a simple (but not simplistic) understanding of two key factors (or 'independent yet related variables') that affect leadership effectiveness. These two factors can be summarised as relating both to people and to the work to be done. A significant number (still possibly the majority) of leadership development approaches offered today can be seen to owe some allegiance to these studies and certainly, at least until the 1990s, this was the dominant base underlying most programmes provided. Alongside this Ohio State leadership studies base, at all times, but probably most obvious from the late 1970s however, research indicated alternative approaches and today there is increasing awareness that leadership is one of the most complex issues with which organisations have to grapple – it's a lot more complex than the interaction of two independent yet related variables.

An important aspect of most leadership approaches is the matter of 'leadership style'. Leadership style can be described as 'the pattern of the leader's behaviour as perceived by others'. In other words, although a leader may use a variety of approaches in his or her interaction with others, there will be a set of behaviours with which he or she is most comfortable and it is these behaviours that others will use to describe the leader when asked. Common descriptive terms that may be used include autocratic, authoritarian, democratic, supportive, etc. When we look at the behaviours of boards in relation to the ethical aspects of corporate governance, it would appear that many use an 'abdicating' style. In other words, they take little or no proactive part in promulgating corporate espoused values by their personal behaviour. They appear to believe that if there is some form of formal statement of values and behaviour then they can leave any modelling and monitoring to those at lower levels in the organisational hierarchy. Given the plethora of ethical lapses with which we are regularly regaled in the media, it is patently obvious that such an approach is having no positive organisational effect and, in fact, can be argued to be deleterious.

The bigger picture

Although much of the leadership material developed in the 1960s and 1970s concentrated on individual leader behaviour, there were always researchers looking at the bigger picture. Among the many of those considering the bigger picture during the 1970s and 1980s were John Adair, James McGregor Burns, Kouzes and Posner and a host of other luminaries.

Although not as widely known as many of his peers during the 1970s, John Adair[5] developed a reputation for his concept of what is known as 'action-centred leadership'. From research that was totally separate from the Ohio University leadership studies, Adair, who was inaugural Professor of Leadership Studies at the University of Surrey in the UK, developed what was essentially a 'whole of organisation' approach. In both its development and in its approach to developing leaders, action-centred leadership explored (and explores) the experiences of a wide range of past and current leaders. This approach recognises the interconnection of management and leadership that is necessary if positive results are to be achieved. Action-centred leadership is an integrated approach to managing and leading. Adair argues that, while leadership and management have much in common, factors such as administration and resource management are specifically 'management' functions, while functions such as inspiring others through the leader's own enthusiasm and commitment are specifically leadership functions. Seeing 'leadership' as the core concept from which 'management' evolved, Adair traced the etymology of leadership to an Anglo-Saxon word meaning the road or path ahead; knowing the next step and then taking others with you on it. He saw the etymology of management as coming from the Latin 'manus', meaning hand, and as being more associated with using a system or machine of some kind. His work argued that to be a more effective leader it was necessary to understand some leadership theory, to be aware of how the three areas of task, group and individual activity interact and to work on the practical applications of general leadership theory in order to select and train leaders effectively. Action-centred leadership presents a holistic approach to individual, group and organisational effectiveness.

In 1978, James McGregor Burns introduced the concept of transformational leadership,[6] which considered the difference between dealing with individuals, groups and entire organisations. Burns argued that, to move forward, many organisations needed to be totally transformed. And he saw this as requiring a completely different approach from the 'transactional' approach of interacting one-with-one or one-with-small-group that tended to dominate in some situational, contingency or other generally used approaches. Other writers also followed up on this concept and works such as John Adams' *Transforming Leadership: From Vision to Results*[7] made valuable contributions to this concept.

In 1987, James M. Kouzes and Barry Z. Posner followed up on this transformational approach in their book *The Leadership Challenge: How to Get Extraordinary Things Done in Organizations.*[8] In this book they argued that there are five key practices to be used in leadership that will bring about and maintain high-performing organisations. These are:

1 Challenging the process
2 Inspiring a shared vision
3 Enabling others to act
4 Modelling the way
5 Encouraging the heart.

Kouzes and Posner argue that, regardless of their position in an organisation, any person can exhibit leadership through implementing these five practices. They make it clear that failure to challenge the status quo in organisations is a failure in leadership because it allows inefficient or outdated processes to continue with a consequent loss of productivity and performance. At the same time, Kouzes and Posner make it clear that it is not enough to see what is wrong with something – it is important to have a vision of how things could be and to communicate that to others in such a way that they, too, become committed to making that vision a reality. As with the situational or contingency approaches, they recognise that these five practices start with the individual, but an important aspect of Kouzes and Posner's work is that, to bring about real organisational transformation, the practices need to be developed and implemented right across the organisation rather than simply in the behaviours of individual leaders.

In 1990 another researcher, Stephen R. Covey,[9] suggested that, rather than focusing on behaviours, the key to effective leadership was to understand and apply a set of universal principles. He saw this process as starting with the individual but, recognising that leadership involved more than just the individual, in Covey's approach, the emphasis then shifted so that the universal principles were applied across four organisational levels – personal, interpersonal, managerial and organisational. He saw these key principles as being:

- trustworthiness at the personal level;
- trust at the interpersonal level;
- empowerment at the managerial level;
- alignment at the organisational level.

Covey makes the point that, unless there is trust at the personal and interpersonal levels of an organisation, a truly high-performing opera-tion is never going to come into existence. There is a very real sense of futility at the lower levels of an organisation when those leading the organisation, either wittingly or unwittingly, create or allow to develop, an atmosphere of suspicion and mistrust. Unless there is a high level of trust across the organisation then even the best intentions of leaders will bear the stigma of possible manipulation, so that 'empowerment' becomes 'second-guessing the boss' and encouragement is ignored or ridiculed – and these are immediate (and usually readily apparent, at least to an outside observer) signs of an organisation in decline. The develop-ment of real trust is often ignored by those ultimately responsible for the organisation's performance. Of course, there is an obvious connection with regard to ethics. If we cannot trust the board of a company to oper-ate in an ethical manner then how can we expect ethical behaviour at any other level in the same organisation? It is becoming increasingly obvious that ethical lapses at the lower levels of an organisation are indicative of a perceived lack of ethics modelling at the very top.

For virtually all organisations, the fact exists that 'what the boss touches is seen to be important' and if the 'boss' seems to think that it's perfectly alright to publically espouse one approach yet model another (and that is inclusive of remuneration issues!), you can be absolutely certain that it is his or her behaviour that will be seen and copied and that the organisation will be nowhere near 'high performing'.

In the first decades of the twenty-first century, we have encoun-tered a situation in which the working hours of Western industrialised countries seem to be increasing. There appears to be an assumption that employees (particularly those in 'white-collar' jobs) should be prepared to work whatever hours are required to meet targets set by their bosses. Very often it seems that those in management and executive positions are expected to be available 168 hours a week (or '24/7') and to have no interests or involvements other than their work. In many ways we seem to have regressed to the situation that pertained over 100 years ago.

From reading newspapers as well as from talking with people, the impression is gained that many people today are scared of taking leave that is due or even of seeking medical and/or dental treatment that might be required because time away from the workplace could be penalised in the next round of layoffs or cost-cutting. We encounter situations in which companies crash, with employees, minor creditors and small stockholders left out of pocket – sometimes while directors, executives, the banks and other major creditors continue to receive their monies due or deemed due because of 'performance' clauses in contracts. In the event of non-executive employees seeking to protect their interests we are still likely to encounter similar anti-union views to those which permeated society in the earlier years of the twentieth century – the workers and their supporters are vilified for daring to want security of entitlements. In other cases, top executives receive salary increases and bonuses after initiating and managing major redundancy waves of employees at lower levels across the organisation.

Then we presume to criticise the ethics and behaviours of people at levels below the board and executive team!

Board leadership

As we have argued consistently, ultimately it is the board that sets the tone for leadership throughout the organisation. Where a board is functioning as a cohesive body – which does *not* mean that disagreement and discussion are at all stifled – then it functions as an effective operating body that is clear about its governance responsibilities and which fully recognises that, ultimately, the success or failure of the organisation rests upon its collective shoulders. As Jeffrey Sachs[10] argued in 2011, it is also the case that the board actually sets the moral and ethical tone for the organisation – if an organisation has moral or ethical lapses (and of recent years we've seen myriad examples of these throughout the world) then it is on the shoulders of the board that the ultimate blame should rest.

One of our roles as academics and consultants is to assist boards to assess their effectiveness. Like most others involved with this activity, we have a series of questionnaires that are answered by each director on a 'peer assessment' basis. From the use of these questionnaires over many years we have developed indicative norms against which the responses can be compared. The full report is provided to the chair and deputy chair while each director receives a report which provides them with their personal information but which does not identify any other set of responses. While all the questions are important for the overall picture, a quick impression can be obtained from responses to questions, in one questionnaire, about general attitude and disposition:

- Provides valuable input on ethics and operations;
- Alert and inquisitive;
- Meeting preparation;
- Long-range planning contribution.

and, in another:

- Attends meetings well prepared to evaluate and/or add value to agenda items presented to the board and/or committee;
- Keeps current on areas and issues on/about which is asked to deliberate and decide;
- Based on contributions made at board meetings, gives the impression of being prepared;
- Has good conceptual and theoretical ability, especially on ethics and operations;
- Supports ongoing change and development.

Some years ago, Sir Adrian Cadbury set out the main functions of a board as being:[11]

- to define the company's purpose;
- to agree the strategies and plans for achieving that purpose;
- to establish the company's policies;
- to appoint the CEO;
- to review the performance of the CEO and the executive team;
- in all this, to be the driving force in the company.

Cadbury also defines the responsibility of the board chairman as being to ensure that the board:

- provides leadership and vision;
- has the right balance of membership;
- sets the aims, strategy and policies of the company;
- monitors the achievement of those aims;
- reviews the resources of people in the company;
- has the information it needs for it to be effective.

Ultimately, the success or failure of an organisation reflects the leadership provided by the board – and especially the chairperson. At this level there has to be a form of leadership that focuses on the long term yet is fully cognisant of the short term; that provides clear parameters within which the executive team can operate and that sets in train a process that will engender engagement and commitment throughout the organisation. The priority of operating in a manner that is both legal *and* ethical should be a core emphasis in this role. Sadly, either because of ignorance, micromanagement, abdication of responsibility or, in the worst case scenarios, moral turpitude, criminal behaviour, ignorance or conflict of interest, far too many boards fail to achieve this crucial goal.

Notes

1 Jacques, E. and Clement, S. (1994) *Executive Leadership: A Practical Guide to Managing Complexity* (with R. Lessem), Blackwell, Oxford.
2 See http://www.smh.com.au/business/retail/slaves-to-the-share-price-legendary-ceo-paul-simons-on-why-woolworths-needs-to-stock-up-on-humble-pie-20160603-gpaygz.html [21 July 2016].
3 Long, D. G. (2012) *Third Generation Leadership and the Locus of Control: Knowledge, Change and Neuroscience*, Gower, UK.
4 One of the best summaries of leadership research and approaches over the years is found in Bass, B. M. and Stogdill, R. M. (1990) *Bass & Stogdill's Handbook of Leadership: Theory, Research, and Managerial Applications*, 3rd edn, The Free Press, New York. More recently, Gary Yukl's book *Leadership in Organizations* (2013), 8th edn, Pearson Education, Harlow, UK provides a contemporary update on the concept.
5 Adair, J. (1983) *Effective Leadership: A Modern Guide to Developing Leadership Skills*, Gower, London.
6 More recent information about this can be found in Burns, J. M. (2003) *Transforming Leadership: A New Pursuit of Happiness*, Atlantic Monthly Press, New York.
7 Adams, J. D. (ed.) (1986) *Transforming Leadership: From Vision to Results*, Miles River Press, VA, USA.
8 Kouzes, J. M. and Posner, B. Z. (1987) *The Leadership Challenge: How to Get Extraordinary Things Done in Organizations*, Jossey-Bass, San Francisco, CA.
9 Covey, S. R. (1990) *Principle-Centered Leadership*, Fireside, New York.
10 Sachs, J. (2011) *The Price of Civilisation: Economics and Ethics after the Fall*, The Bodley Head, Random House, London.
11 Cadbury, Sir A. (1995) *The Company Chairman*, Director Books, UK.

Part II

The board's role in corporate ethics

5 The board's macro perspective

In February 2016, Knowledge@Wharton released the first of a series of special reports on business ethics.[1] This report concentrated on business ethics as a means of enhancing corporate governance and drew a clear distinction between the purpose of an organisation – its raison d'être – and its mission (what an organisation actually does). It argued that, until the directors of an organisation actually understand why the organisation exists, why it needs to exist, why would it be missed if it didn't exist and what would be missing in the world were it not for the organisation, then actually deciding what an organisation should do and how it should act is futile. When the board has clear answers to these questions, then proper corporate governance – the phenomenon of action-guiding – becomes possible and true corporate governance can be achieved.

Consider again the set of anecdotes with which we started this book. Do these sound as though they come from organisations that have really considered their raison d'être? Some are consistent with a perspective which argues that the purpose of an organisation is to make money and such a view is inconsistent with any perspective which holds that an organisation has (and actually needs) a greater purpose in order to set it apart from its competitors.

The Knowledge@Wharton report states that research by the Gallup Organisation shows that, worldwide, only about 13 per cent of employees are truly engaged with their employer (the United States has one of the highest rates at 30 per cent) which means that some 87 per cent of people across all organisational levels are effectively carrying out their work to a standard that is well below what could be achieved. And a prime reason for this lack of engagement is unethical behaviour – although organisations may claim in their publicity that 'employees are our greatest asset' (or some sentiment akin to this), in fact in some cases the only people who are really seen as being important are those at the top – and even they are sometimes expendable. There is a disconnect between what the organisation says and what it actually does – and it is the behaviour we see that gives rise to the opinions we form about any organisation.

Zivit always advises managers to remember that employees are in continuous observation mode. They watch what managers choose to do and not to do, observe day-to-day behaviours, hear what managers say and analyse what is not being said, evaluate managerial decisions and note when decisions are not being made. Employees look at the entire management team (including the board), not only at their own manager. Often managers respond negatively to this statement. They think that employees pay attention only to major events. However, it is the day-to-day behaviours that employees most closely monitor – when managers arrive at work, how they behave, etc. Employees are the first to detect gaps between the stated values and organisational culture and the reality of the company's ethos. These gaps always stem from the top management behaviour. This is how the disconnect evolves; this is how unethical practices develop.

The Knowledge@Wharton report quotes Professor Thomas Donaldson of the Wharton Business School as suggesting that the purpose of business 'has to be seen as a form of cooperation involving production, distribution and exchange for the purpose of creating collective value'. It is very clear that this does not negate competition – using a sporting analogy, the report shows that for overall competition to be effective there needs to be significant internal cooperation in each team. A quick look at the behaviour of organisations in almost every country makes it clear that some organisations don't seem to get the message either about cooperation or about the need to establish organisational purpose.

Of course, the way in which organisational purpose is actually expressed by individual companies will vary significantly. The Wharton report cites, among other examples, the purpose of Ethos Water (now owned by Starbucks) as 'bringing fresh water to parts of the world that don't have it'; the purpose of Alibaba in China as to 'make a better China'; Steve Jobs of Apple's purpose as wanting 'to put a dent in the universe'; Warby Parker Spectacles' purpose as showing that 'everyone has the right to see'; LinkedIn's purpose as 'allowing everybody who has talent to have that talent recognised'. All these organisations are profitable, successful operations. The point being made is that having a very clear purpose that is far broader than 'making money' frames the entire organisation in a different manner and this different manner both sets the scene for ethical corporate governance and creates a corporate identity to which employees can become committed. In other words, argues the Wharton report, setting a clear purpose enhances the probability of ethical conduct throughout the organisation, enhances the probability of employee engagement and, in turn, this enhances the probability of enhanced profits.

If corporate governance is all about what an organisation should be doing, then developing and promulgating an organisational purpose sets the scene for the most comprehensive and effective corporate governance possible because it helps people find meaning in their work – and that is central to people doing things properly. Quoting Henrik Syse, a senior research fellow at Peace Research Institute in Oslo, Norway, the report goes on to say (p. 5) 'once we open ourselves to the possibility that the purpose of a firm goes beyond mere profit-making, we also introduce a crucial element of ethical thinking into the heart of corporate governance'.

In terms of the Johari Window, what determining and promulgating a clear organisational purpose does is to enable a larger arena (that area that is known to both oneself and to others) to emerge.

It is now almost a given for most organisations that, ultimately, long-term competitive advantage is found in one's people. If an organisation wants to be seen as ethical and believes that this will give them a competitive edge, then it needs to create an environment in which its people act in an ethical manner and this requires all of the information the organisation provides and all of the feedback it receives to positively emphasise ethical standards of behaviour in every context. And the board needs to model ethical behaviour.

So how can it do this?

Professor Zeynep Ton of Massachusetts Institute of Technology (MIT) argues that the enlarging of a positive organisational arena starts with the way the organisation treats its people.[2] She demonstrates that ensuring that staff are not overworked, are well paid and receive relatively high levels of staff benefits results in higher employee engagement, lower employee turnover, higher employee productivity, improved levels of innovation and better results for the organisation. She also argues that this is an ethical issue because, by demonstrating high levels of care for its people, an organisation makes it clear that it is genuinely driven by a desire to provide services rather than by cost cutting in order to maximise profits. The point being made is that, when it comes to ethics, the way an organisation is assessed is by what people see and hear about the organisation. If an organisation is broadly seen as a good place to work, then it tends to be recognised as operating in an ethical manner.

The bigger context

As already indicated, while laws and regulations make it clear what we must or must not do, ethics is all about what we ought to do. And here

Table 1 The business conundrum

	Organisational goals	Societal goals
Ethics	The Ethical Conservative Organisation	The Conscious Societal Organisation
Laws/regulations	The Conservative Organisation	The Compliant Societal Organisation

lies the conundrum. As Clare Graves made clear,[3] if we have differing world views then we will also have differing views as to what we ought to do. Consequently, as we consider the issue of values, ethics and corporate governance, it is important to realise that, no matter how much one might want to be prescriptive, we are not dealing with 'black and white' issues but with a very wide range of 'grey shades'. Putting it very simply, it can be argued that the business conundrum is to maintain an appropriate balance between ethics and law, between organisational goals and societal goals. This concept is illustrated in Table 1.

Using this framework, the conservative approach – which reflects the current corporate governance system (emphasising short-term company revenues while complying with the relevant local laws) – tends to dominate. When laws are less restrictive in a different country and there is an opportunity to gain revenues or reduce production and operation costs, it is considered totally acceptable to transfer business operations as long as there is legal compliance. This practice is widely seen in such areas as mining companies from developed countries operating in developing countries and also in much of the outsourcing of manufacturing by organisations in the clothing and footwear industries.

However, the ethical conservative approach moves beyond simple compliance with law and considers organisational profit from the ethical perspective. For example, is it ethical to employ children in countries where it is legal to do so simply in order to reduce production costs? In other words, does the end (optimising profit) ever justify the means (exploiting children) in the quest for organisational success?

The Compliant Societal Organisation represents an organisation which is looking beyond its purely short-term goals, but still via the legal lens. In other words, the organisation is clearly focused on its long-term viability but is doing so within a framework that considers only 'what is legal'.

The Conscious Societal Organisation represents the space in which organisations should operate in order to survive in the long term. Organisations operating in this quadrant not only consider the environment and the societies within which they operate, but also ask in every situation what they ought to do in order to bring about short- and long-term benefits not only for the organisation in question but also for the country in which it operates and for the people who work for it, both directly and indirectly.

In order to move into the societal zones, boards must change their conservative way of operating. Such a shift in corporate stance needs to include structural changes (committees and what they focus on), ensuring diversity of thoughts and actively bringing ethics, environment, society and technology to the forefront of decision making.

What the framework of Table 1 suggests is that, in the running of a business, directors and managers will need to find a way of meeting the sometimes (but not always) competing demands of their ambitions and society and of operating in a manner that is both ethical and within the law. In finding this balance they will be guided by their own world view or, in Gravesian[4] terms, their personal value system.

When we raise this issue of 'values' it is important to realise that we are not talking of the sorts of 'values' that are espoused in so many organisational statements. James Adonis addresses this in part when he asks the question: 'Do corporate values matter?'[5] In this article he refers to research published in the *Journal of Financial Economics*[6] which, after studying some 500 businesses, concluded that there was no automatic correlation between the declaration of an organisation's values in either the short term or the long term. As stated elsewhere,[7] a key reason for this is that, in the main, 'values statements' tend to be generic statements that are open to broad interpretation and which, generally, can be (and are) used to justify any action whether or not it is ethical and, all too often, whether or not it is legal. That is why, in *Delivering High Performance*, the recommendation is made to express all values statements in behavioural terms so that there is a direct link between what an organisation publically espouses and what is actually done. It is also why we are now drawing a clear distinction between 'organisational values' and the 'values' (or 'world views') discussed by Beck and Cowan.[8] It is your world views that will determine how you interpret and enact those values that form 'organisational values statements' in their common form.

Another point to remember here is that, unfortunately, all too often the organisational values that are exhibited on the company's walls and website are not adhered to in practice. The abovementioned case of VW is illustrative of this. In many cases, it is the leadership that fails to model these values. They talk the talk but don't walk the walk. This, in itself, sends a negative ethical message to employees. Employees see these behaviours daily; for boards it is sometimes more difficult to notice.

Businesses exist primarily to make money. An entrepreneur starts with an idea, sees a commercial possibility and seeks to exploit that opportunity for financial gain. There is absolutely nothing wrong with this – in fact it is essential for economic success – and it has been the case since time immemorial. Laws and regulations address the more blatant problems associated with an 'end justifies the means' approach but the very fact of business being profit orientated means that there is always some aspect of 'the end justifies the means' in every business. It is futilely idealistic to suggest that business could operate in any other way because 'profit' (in one form or another) is the core building block of every economy, whether capitalistic or otherwise.

As we hope is becoming clear, it is the means by which 'profit' is obtained that is the concern of ethics.

Over the years much has been said and written on ethics from both philosophic and religious perspectives. The 'golden rule' (do unto others as you would have done unto yourself) is broadly encompassed by virtually all philosophic systems (especially the Kantian) and religious faiths. But while this may be an admirable concept, in practice its application is either often ignored or reinterpreted to permit a wide range of actions.

Virtually all those running organisations recognise that they have to balance profit imperatives with legal and social responsibilities. There is, however, sometimes a blurring of the line between 'legal' and 'ethical'. As already indicated, for many people the question is never one of ethics – their world view is such that, providing they are operating within legal boundaries, their actions must also be ethical. This is especially the case when their observations indicate that this is how their peers also operate.

The questions relating to ethical behaviour are centred on issues such as:

- ethical issue intensity (How important is the ethical issue in the eyes of the individual, group or organisation?); and
- consideration of the cognitive state of the person making the decision (Can they appreciate that it is unethical?).

When we consider these issues in relation to the behaviour seen in many organisations then the thing that comes clear is that, in relation to differences between what we ought to do from a legal perspective and what we ought to do from a moral perspective, the issue intensity tends to be low. If our core value system is primarily focused on maximising profit through legal competitive behaviour, then tax minimisation through transfer pricing and related practices is totally legitimate, regardless of any negative social impacts it may have. The same is true for employment of people on lowest rate casual contracts that provide no long-term security of employment or benefits in terms of paid leave, sickness, retirement, etc. Along with this, because such actions are totally legal, then matters such as cognitive knowledge simply do not arise. It is not until pressure is applied (usually from some third-party source) that moral intensity is increased and a degree of urgency emerges in answering questions such as:

- Has the organisation set clear values or guiding principles?
- Are the organisational rules of ethical conduct clear?

In answering these questions, organisations are then forced to confront other issues relating to such matters as corporate culture (including policies and actual leadership on ethics as well as opportunities for unethical behaviour); behaviours of significant others at work (including peer groups, leadership and managers) and the extent of obedience to authority that is expected of all employees.

But even if questions such as this do exist, the answer as to appropriate behaviour may still not be clear.

Although businesses are there to make a profit, they still have social responsibility. This means, not only commit no harm, but also try to do good.

In the course on ethics and competitive advantage at the Australian School of Business, UNSW, one of the classes involves showing an Australian Broadcasting Corporation recording of a 2011 investigative study of asbestos.[9] This course attracts a very broad range of students from both Australia and internationally. A number of these international students come from developing countries and so see things a little differently from their developed country student peers. Invariably these students from developing countries point out that this study raises two quite distinct ethical issues: first is the issue about the manufacture and use of asbestos products in India where it provides both jobs and shelter; second is the issue of Canada mining asbestos for export to India when its use is banned in Canada. On the second issue there is widespread agreement that mining and exporting asbestos – a proven cause of serious health problems – while certainly legal, is almost certainly not ethical. But the first issue is more complex. Yes, it causes health issues and these are well documented and, yes, both the Indian importers and the Government seem to be ignoring health facts. However, in a country where there is little if any social welfare, high unemployment among an army of unskilled workers and extreme poverty, this industry provides, along with inexpensive building materials, jobs and money when, otherwise, existence may be scarcely possible. This, recently argued one of Doug's students, means that, based on the economic good it is doing for these disadvantaged people, the production and use of asbestos-based products by the Indian manufacturer is ethical. However, responded the rest of the class, today's problems are often the result of yesterday's solutions. In this case, a short-term solution for providing work is almost certainly creating a major long-term problem for both India and the individuals working in the factories and using the products. In the meantime, the owners of the business are maximising their profits through activities that exploit the most vulnerable and, by almost any standard, such behaviour, although understandable, is unethical. Distinguishing between the Canadian miner and exporter and the Indian manufacturer and product supplier is disingenuous. Their conclusion was that there is no corporate ethical behaviour in this case study – all parties are operating unethically.

In many ways, this example highlights the conflict existing between the economic rationalist[10] view of organisations and the socio-economic view of organisations. The economic rationalist argues that the primary responsibility of directors and managers is to ensure that the best interests of the shareholders are served and, further, that as the best interests of the shareholders relate to return on their investment, anything that reduces (or has the potential to reduce) returns to shareholders is inappropriate managerial behaviour. Under this approach, the actions of the companies both in Canada and in India would be considered justified as the owners of the various companies benefit from the profits obtained. The socio-economic view argues that businesses are no longer simply economic institutions (and questions whether they ever were). Given the reality that many multinational companies are financially larger than a significant number of independent countries, there is an increasing expectation that businesses will become heavily involved in social, political and legal issues. For example, right across the globe, finance, mining and defence orientated companies exert considerable pressure on national governments because of the numbers of people employed and the contribution they make to that nation's GDP. This degree of influence, argue the socio-economic proponents, brings with it a responsibility to act in accordance with the highest moral principles – to ensure their activities are both legal *and* ethical. This means, they continue, that directors and managers must not only produce profits for their shareholders but also protect and improve society's welfare.

The socio-economic view seems to be gaining ground. On Saturday 24 October 2015 the *Canberra Times* carried a newspaper article[11] discussing the way in which shareholder activism is now impacting on the way that companies operate. The author, Sally Rose, argues that shareholder revolts are now utilising both traditional avenues and social media to garner support for their cause and this is combining with 'ethical investor organisations' to pressure boards into conforming with socio-economic standards. They argue that socially responsible investment is today's imperative and that part of this socially responsible investment involves withdrawing their funds from companies that are operating in industries which have a negative impact on individuals and the environment. Rose also points out that the regulatory authorities in Australia seem to have no serious concerns about the rise of this pressure movement.

But what is the relationship between corporate social responsibility and corporate ethics? The link is that both tell us something about the culture of an organisation. If an organisation is dominated by an economic rationalist culture – in other words the board and management believe that their primary responsibility is solely to maximise returns to their shareholders – it is reasonable to assume that any focus on corporate social responsibility is more illusionary than actual and that in fact, even if not in theory, an 'the end justifies the means' culture will exist. This was alluded to in the *New York Times* when, in relation to corporate ethical behaviour, it was stated:

> Both Volkswagen and BP were trying to win customers by joining the 93 per cent of Fortune 250 companies that report how well they treat the environment. They promise that they care about our community, our future. But too often corporate social responsibility reports are nothing more than public relations exercises with little substance.[12]

As already stated, the culture of an organisation exerts significant influence on the behaviour of employees at all levels – from the CEO down – and that culture is ultimately set by the board. As has been said elsewhere:[13]

> If a company is successful it is due to the efforts of everyone in it, but if it fails it is because of the failure of the board. If the board fails it is the responsibility of the chairman, notwithstanding the collective responsibility of everyone. Despite this collective responsibility, it is on the chairman's shoulders that the competition and the performance of that supreme directing body depends.

If an organisation's culture is based on sound values that support corporate social responsibility and high ethical standards and those values are expressed in behavioural terms, then a strong culture that inculcates those values will eventually emerge. In turn, this strong culture will have a very powerful and positive influence on how people throughout the organisation act in their pursuit of optimum returns for their shareholders – which leads to a further consideration, discussed below.

Complexity and ambiguity

There are many people who believe that strategy is solely the domain of executive management. They argue that those who are best able to determine the direction of an organisation are those who are closest to it in terms of operational expertise and responsibility. But the main problem with this premise is that the executive team very often has a relatively short-term, partly self-interested focus on where an organisation should go and how it should get there. They are 'hired guns' who, so it seems, stay for a relatively short time (about three to five years on average) in an organisation before moving on to new challenges and, in this period, their remuneration is usually closely tied to the results achieved by the organisation during their period of tenure. There is nothing wrong with this 'hired guns' concept, as all organisations need regular infusions of new thinking and new approaches if they are to avoid stagnation and the right turnover of executives can help to ensure innovation and growth. However, there is an obvious conflict for executives (with a relatively short-term focus on what can and will be achieved within a three- to five-year time frame) and the long-term benefits to the organisation's owners – the shareholders – through the long-term viability of an organisation. This concern was indirectly raised by Shields, O'Donnell and O'Brien[14] of the universities of Sydney, Canberra and New South Wales, respectively, whose research indicated that the long-term performance of a company can deteriorate in direct relation to increases in executive remuneration.

Much of this conflict is resolved when the board accepts ultimate responsibility for direction and strategy because directors of a company do not experience this same conflict. The legal requirement of directors is that they answer to the company as a distinct legal entity or 'person' and they look after the interests of all shareholders (including the smallest stockholders) as their primary responsibility. Directors receive set fees and are not on performance-related bonuses that depend on results achieved in any particular period. Certainly, if an organisation is considered by its shareholders to be underperforming, the board can be replaced and directors (along with executives) are often themselves stockholders, but the law is clear about the difference between governance and executive responsibilities. Accordingly, the board can and should provide the checks and balances to ensure that executive self-interest doesn't impact the longer term interests of the company.

Of course, this level of oversight does not always result in appropriate behaviour. Ross Gittins, an Australian economic journalist, addressed this issue when stating that economic theorists and government bureaucrats, in arguing for competition to be the arbiter of appropriate behaviour, fail to fully realise the potentially destructive power of the profit motive.[15] He points out that there is strong evidence to support the contention that business can be so highly motivated by short-term profits that both boards and executives 'play the system' and are always looking for loop-holes and ways of bending the rules in order to achieve financial results. Their activities may be legal but questions relating to their ethics are certainly justified.

For many years, research by Elliott Jaques (referred to in Chapter 4) indicated that the most successful organisations ensure that people at all levels have the appropriate degree of capability to deal with the extent of ambiguity and complexity that is demanded from their level of respon-sibility. He argues that those at the very top of organisations should have the conceptual abstract capability of 20+ years,[16] meaning that they should be alert to and preparing for any possible contingency that may emerge. To meet this requirement, the board needs to be focused on the long term of 20+ years while also remaining receptive to what is happening in the short term.

For one of his birthdays, Doug's family gave him a rally car driv-ing experience. At a designated rally driving school location in the Australian bush, he was first given lessons in rally car driving and then was required to drive over two courses in which he encountered the full range of conditions faced by professional car rally contestants. Right from the start his instructor, a very successful Australian rally car driver, emphasised that the secret to optimising rally times lay in concentrating on the furthest point visible while never losing sight of what was immediately in front of the car's bonnet. After some trial and error, Doug achieved times that were considered reasonable and then he was offered the opportunity for a 'fast lap' experience. Swapping seats with the instructor, Doug held on for dear life as his instructor flew around the circuit at speeds well in excess of anything Doug could attain. Afterwards the instructor made the point that, with his years of experience, he was able not only to focus on the furthest possible point visible but that he could also imagine what may lie beyond that point and he was, at all times, preparing himself for what might be encoun-tered at the same time as dealing with the present.

There is an analogy here for boards. By the time a person is appointed to a board they generally have years of experience in professional and/or executive roles – sometimes with the organisation to whose board they are now appointed. The reason they are appointed is that they are believed to have practical and conceptual skills that are greater than those in executive management. They need to be able to supply a 'value-add' to what the executive team are able to do. This 'value-add' is not found in replicating the work of the executive management nor in checking on what the executive team do or how they do it. It is found in creating the macro environment in which the executive team can lead the organisation so that it prospers in both the short and the long term. The board provides this 'value-add' by focusing on the furthest possible point visible (at least 20 years in the future), and using their experience and intuition to anticipate and prepare for contingencies far beyond the most comprehensive plans being implemented. The executive team may focus on their five- (or so) year plan. The board should be preparing the company for what lies well beyond.

Unfortunately, experience indicates that many boards are simply not up to this task. If the board resiles from its strategic responsibilities and concentrates primarily on supervising the activities of executives, they are effectively allowing those executives to determine both where the organisation is going and how it will get there. Under such conditions the board is not creating the optimal environment for organisational success and they are not using their knowledge and intuition to help the executive team prepare for and confront any possible contingency. It is possible that they are not even meeting the full extent of their legal responsibilities (let alone their ethical responsibilities) in relation to shareholders.

There is a clear implication here for ethics.

When James Hardie Industries decided to move its operations from Australia to the Netherlands, did the initiative come from the executive team or the board? When supermarkets decided to limit what they would pay suppliers for vegetables and fruit, did the initiative come from the executive team or the board? If the initiative came from the executive team and the board failed to consider the wider implications (i.e. other than the impact on the short-term 'bottom line') then it is possible that the board were not demonstrating the degree of strategic foresight that was appropriate. Of course, if the initiative came from the board then even more questions arise!

So far, we have argued that a board's responsibility is to:

- establish the strategic goals and direction for the organisation;
- determine and monitor the culture of an organisation;
- determine and demonstrate the values for the organisation;
- set and demonstrate the ethical imperatives for the organisation;

and that, in doing this, through the exercise of their greater ability to deal with ambiguity and complexity, they provide a clear 'value-add' to whatever is done by the executive.

Clearly, Ray Anderson in the Interface example provided above (Chapter 2) recognised this and, as a result, the means by which Interface achieves its goals is significantly different today from what it was prior to 1997. They have found a competitive advantage through ensuring that their espoused values are also their implemented values.

On 7 November 2015, the weekend edition of Knowledge@ Wharton included an article entitled 'The power of treating employees like family'[17] in which the chairman of a highly successful US company, Barry-Wehmiller, explained that the process of transforming a very old and established but only marginally successful company to its current position of strength occurred primarily because the board was able to see a different way of operating that accepted the past but focused on the future. Rather than being controlled by their current activities, they considered emerging technologies and how these could become the core of tomorrow's business. Their ability to deal with ambiguity and complexity led them to determine new strategic goals and pathways, as well as value systems that would be appropriate in the future rather than remaining with those that had served in the past.

And this is what a board's macro perspective ought to be all about.

An important side-track is needed here. We are talking about two different yet related macro approaches of which a board needs to be cognisant. These are, first, the macro environment in which the board operates – the national and international regulatory and competitive environments within which their company operates – and, second, the macro approach that the board has to take in order to optimise the long-term viability of their company. It is when a board faces the question of 'what ought we to do', that these two different yet related macro concepts come into joint focus.

But before one can ask 'what ought we to do?' from a moral perspective, we need to be very clear about where we are going, how we will get there, the values that will guide our behaviour and the culture we want to exist throughout the organisation.

In the late 1980s, the New South Wales State Government decided that electricity supply in the State could be provided more efficiently if various publically owned retail electricity suppliers were merged and corporatised. In 1989, the bill forming Sydney Electricity (the first of the new entities) was passed, bringing together three local authorities with adjoining borders. When, in 1991, Sydney Electricity became an actuality, almost the first action of the new Chairman, Mr Allan Moyes, was to take the newly appointed board and the executive team to a three-day retreat where they could determine the future of the new organisation. He was very aware that, even on the board, there was not totally uncritical acceptance of the new entity and that merging different cultures and work practices would not be easy – especially given that many duplicated roles would be rationalised and that there would be subsequent job losses. Doug acted as facilitator at this retreat and for the last two days of the retreat the board was joined by the full executive team led by the Chief Executive, Allan Gillespie.

The starting point for this joint meeting was to consider the world as it would be in the twenty-first century. What would the customer demographic be? What would they need? Who would the major competitors be? What new technologies would be available? How could these technologies be harnessed and utilised for commercial purposes? These were the sort of questions addressed as the participants grappled with ambiguity and complexities that could impact in the future. It quickly became apparent that the future would require an emphasis on energy in its broadest forms (such as water, gas, solar, wind, home-located water-based fuel cells, wireless and telecommunication services, etc.) rather than simply a focus on electrical energy. From this broad picture, they then determined the business in which they would be operating and the values that would guide its operations. This led to a clear picture of what the organisation would look like in 1995 and the determination of the culture that the new organisation would need to develop.

The name 'Sydney Electricity' was changed in 1995 to 'Energy Australia' and some years later the corporatised entity was privatised and sold by the then NSW Government. However, during the time that Allan Moyes was Chairman and Allan Gillespie was CEO, there was a strong emphasis on operating in a way that reflected the values determined at that first meeting. Both men were determined that Sydney Electricity should operate in a way that was within both the letter and the spirit of the law as well as being totally ethical. They consistently referred back to the output of the 1991 retreat (and then to the subsequent 1993 retreat) in order to reaffirm both the direction and the modus operandi of the organisation. They got the macro perspective right for the board and this enabled everything else to come together in a way that both gave them an entrée into new operations and was an exemplar of probity.[18]

Sydney Electricity, of course, was in many ways a 'greenfield' site for such an approach. But the story of Interface, referred to in Chapter 2, is another example of this macro perspective driving change in both operational focus and modus operandi. Interface was not being forced into any form of merger or new form. It was a successful, well-established operation that, by many measures, had little or no incentive for significant change. However, once Ray Anderson and the board embraced the implications of the challenging question asked by an executive, it enabled a new perspective to emerge and a totally new operation to evolve.

This highlights the power of the board to get things right from a macro perspective.

As anyone who has done even high school physics knows, Newton's first law of motion states, in effect, that a body will remain at rest or continue in uniform motion in a straight line unless it is acted on by an external force. In the corporate world it means that executives will continue to run an organisation in its existing manner unless there is some pressure to change. Accordingly, most societies (at least Western ones) rightly argue that all businesses should operate in a competitive environment. We have done this reasonably well in terms of product and service innovation and development, product quality, reducing costs and other profit-enhancing activities. The time is well past, however, when we should also do this in terms of ethical behaviour. We need to ensure that both the means and the end are morally compatible. As the examples from Sydney Electricity and Interface show, it is the board's macro perspective that can provide this 'external force'.

The concept of spiral dynamics, to which we have already referred in Chapter 2, makes it clear that value systems only change when people realise that their existing way of operating is not able to meet current and future exigencies. At that point the options are to continue doing the same thing despite experiencing ever-increasing frustration, to pause and consider the options or to embrace the possibility of operating in a new and more comprehensive manner. When the board fully embraces its macro perspective responsibility these three options become apparent and informed choice becomes possible.

So, from a macro perspective, what are the issues that a board should confront?

The issue of humanity

Margaret Thatcher, when Prime Minister of the United Kingdom, is reputed to have stated that 'we live in an economy, not a society'[19] and this economic rationalist thinking has permeated politics and business for at least the past 30 years. Ultimately, it lies behind the activities that have led to many of the 'booms and busts' of the late twentieth and early twenty-first centuries. The only thing that really matters is profit and wealth for the few, even though such possibilities as 'the trickle-down effect' may be outwardly lauded. As has been argued by many researchers,[20] however, there is very little (if any) empirical evidence that this 'trickle-down effect', while much loved and advocated by the executives who reap large benefits, ever actually benefits the company.

It is this approach of believing we live in an economy rather than a society that leads to companies researching a sample (for example, wealthy and powerful people or only people from certain selected countries) and assuming that the research result will apply to humanity overall (i.e. the majority of people). One chairman encapsulated this in saying:

> We are living in an unethical world. We promote consumerism, 5 per cent of the population suffers from addictions. Yet, we take profit from casinos, we commercially exploit holidays (Easter, Christmas, etc.).

Underlying this approach is the work of Milton Friedman (1976 Nobel Prize winner for economics) who advocated a free market economic system with minimal controls.[21] He believed that competitive forces would ensure the best results for everyone – lower prices through competition coupled with better returns to investors through lower operating costs. The central emphasis of business, in Friedman's view, is to make money for its shareholders – a view that has been challenged by a variety of people and, quite recently, by Steve Denning[22] who, in a 2013 article in *Forbes* magazine, claimed that Friedman was simply picking and choosing among legal realities in order to support his own views and hypotheses. Denning argues that Friedman claimed executives are ultimately employees of a corporation's shareholders and that, therefore, they owe allegiance only to the shareholders. However, Denning goes on, in fact executives are employees of their corporation (a separate legal entity from its shareholders) and their primary allegiance is to the corporation per se. This then creates a far more complex responsibility than simply answering to shareholders – all stakeholders, including every employee, suppliers, customers, competitors and society, itself have a vested interest in an organisation's long-term viability and must be considered. It is the greater human factor and not just the financial returns that are actually of primary importance. The implication of this is that creating shareholder wealth is only one of the factors impacting on executive attitudes and behaviour. Denning uses such luminaries as Jack Welch of General Electric, Kenneth Mason of Quaker Oats and management guru, Professor Peter Drucker, to reinforce his argument that many of the problems faced today have been caused by this myopic emphasis on shareholder returns rather than long-term organisational viability.

It is a truism to state that, without its people, an organisation is literally nothing. Yet, time and again, this seems to be forgotten. The resultant disequilibrium between employment categories, status and remuneration can create disharmony and dysfunctional conflict that is epitomised by a 'them and us' attitude between management and non-management personnel. Under such circumstances many people opt for unionisation. There is often an underlying criticism of the trade union movement simply on the basis that it exists. This criticism, however, fails to give any consideration to the significant power imbalance that creates the atmosphere in which people feel the need for such a body. When criminality and abuse is uncovered in specific unions or by specific union leaders, there tends to be an 'I told you so' chorus that condemns trade unions per se rather than simply focusing on the specific parties involved. (That we tend to be far more forgiving of managers, directors and corporations is repeatedly illustrated when we accept, and rightly so, that unethical and/or illegal behaviour uncovered in specific organisa-tions does not indicate that this is endemic across all organisations.) This denigration of unions and their activities becomes even more vehement should employees have the audacity to limit or withdraw their labour in order to redress any perceived imbalance in bargaining positions when addressing such issues as remuneration, safety, etc. In our current busi-ness model it seems that the quest to keep costs to a minimum requires that those within the lower echelons of organisations receive the bare minimum while those at the top can receive the rewards to which they believe they are entitled. This can be a recipe for short-term success at the cost of long-term viability.

Of course, questionable practices are not confined to the management of organisations. There are many examples of unethical practices and behaviours by trade unions as well. Sometimes it is the unions that take a controversially unethical route. For example, recently a trade union in Victoria demanded a 20 per cent salary increase for all the public sector employees over the next four years (5 per cent a year – which is way above the consumer price index) and an increase in annual leave days from 20 to 25 (stating that the current allocation makes it diffi-cult for public sector employees to spend the summer holidays at home with their children). Ultimately, it is the private sector that would have to carry the burden if such measures were adopted and the argument that public sector employees should get more leave is unethical. Can an ethical union (which is an organisation) grow and operate ethically within an organisation that adopts unethical practices? Can we have an ethical board dealing with an unethical union? It is important to realise that unions and trade unions are organisations themselves with their own goals and agendas. Accordingly, their directors and managers are just as likely as those from any other type of organisation to fall into the trap of unethical behaviour.

The fact is that people are vital to organisations. Goods and services are, ultimately, purchased by people and, again ultimately, it is people who create these. All directors and employees have an obligation to do what is best for the organisation (both legally and ethically) so as to ensure both its short-term and long-term success. Research shows that such viability is best achieved when people at all levels are working in harmony towards a common goal – there is organisational attunement as well as alignment between the 'hard' and 'soft' aspects of the organisation. Ultimately, as the saying goes, 'disharmony is death'. We cannot pretend that only the economy is important. The economy is a vital tool of humanity – it may even be one of the glues that hold societies together – but its essence is people.

The issue of the world changing a lot quicker than the old systems of governance

When we are regaled by so many and such frequent accounts of corporations behaving badly, it is clear that the legal system within which boards operate is lagging behind social and technological changes. The ethical framework that boards rely on also hasn't changed over the past few decades, even though society itself seems to demanding new standards. From the board's perspective there is a temptation to believe that the only change seems to be that, as one chairperson put it at interview, 'the goal post moved and the penalty for reputation is greater' rather than realising that the world in which they operate today is vastly different from the one that was extant as recently as just last century.

The corporate governance system today still allows organisations to:

- focus on the short term – without being concerned with future generations and society at large;
- be centred on the shareholder and maximise shareholder return ('instead of adding value to the world');
- channel wealth from those who produce goods and services to those who find creative ways of shifting paper without actually producing anything tangible;
- take without giving back (for example, in distribution of dividends, share buy-back options);
- distribute selective information without full transparency.

As one chairman said:

> We need to reinvent the relationships between business and society, if we want to achieve social sustainability.

It is natural for humans to be self-centred. Like all other animals, our most basic instinct is for survival and that requires us to pay attention to those things that affect our existence. But humans are both similar and dissimilar to other animals. Abilities such as thinking conceptually, planning and discerning right from wrong set us apart and are important here.

We have already referred to the issue of social responsibility and the rise of pressure groups claiming the moral high ground on such issues, but emerging concepts regarding governance are broader than this. There is increasing concern globally about governments (which, at least in democratic countries, are ultimately accountable to their people) outsourcing such matters as security and immigration services, aspects of police and prison services, many health and education administration services, infrastructure design, construction and management and the like to private enterprise organisations that have no public accountability. When those with great wealth exploit such legal measures as offshore companies and a variety of trusts to grow and manage their wealth, then further pressure-group scrutiny regarding what they are doing and how they operate is inevitable. As reported in the *Sydney Morning Herald* on 7 December 2015,[23] under these conditions it is not surprising that issues such as wealth disparity and racial divides receive attention, with calls for changes to systems which perpetuate such matters.

These sorts of issues are raising new concerns for company directors. Once it was possible to provide governance by ensuring that the organisation operated within appropriate legal and professional constraints. At one time a company's annual report was signed off by the auditors, the chair and the CEO as providing an accurate picture of the state of the organisation and, while providing extensive financial detail, issues such as board and executive remuneration were private matters. Then it became necessary to provide information about this remuneration. Once the societal impact of an organisation's operations was not considered important public information but, today, even though such information is not mandated, many organisations are finding that reporting on this is viewed positively.

The world in which organisations operate is changing fast. Boards need to adapt – and quickly – to the new reality. The point here is that we cannot expect individual boards to adapt until the corporate system itself changes. Boards are trapped between operating according to an outdated corporate governance system, including laws, and the rapid societal and technological changes in the world.

The issue of technology

As both Sydney Electricity and Interface discovered, rapid technological advancements challenge the board and put ethics centre stage. Customers and stakeholders can now voice their views with potentially damaging effects on reputation. The board meets once a month, but on social media whatever they discuss is already ancient history.

Worldwide, the development of technology runs far ahead of legislation. Disruptive technological advancements are confronting virtually every business and, too often, company directors lag behind their management in understanding the implication of these and their impact on governance – even if their management team has already considered this. But even when directors do understand the practicalities of new technologies, the wider conceptual issue of the impact on governance may not even appear on their horizons because, in the main, they are (totally understandably) focused on meeting the current legal requirements of governance and, especially if a director holds multiple directorships, finding time to reflect on more esoteric questions simply may not be either a priority or even possible.

As with Sydney Electricity, the management team needs to take the lead in sourcing and implementing technological advances but it is imperative that they keep their board informed about what is available and what could become available in the future. The board is then responsible for considering the ethical and other governance issues concerning the availability and utilisation of these technologies and it is critical that they consider these before the management team brings recommendations for their purchase.

Governing and directing ethics: varying and complementary roles of boards

With changes in societal norms, there is a corresponding movement of ethical boundaries. In the past, boardrooms were occupied by members of the old school tie brigade. That was (and, in many cases, still is) the practice. It wasn't unethical, but it didn't take the broader view into account. Today, with society changing in favour of diversity of thoughts, social inclusion and gender balance, the previous practice becomes old-fashioned and is seen by some as unethical.

In today's management reality we see a trend of higher societal interest in the ethical behaviour of organisations. The bar of societal expectations is on the rise. While the corporate governance system is built on share-holders' benefits, society expects sustainability and social awareness.

This is the issue faced by organisations such as James Hardie Industries. There were no ethical barriers to the mining, utilisation and marketing of asbestos during the 1930s, and even in the 1960s, when concerns did emerge, there was no strong ethical pressure demanding that action be taken. However when, finally, the excreta hit the air-conditioning the then current board were judged by twenty-first century ethical stand-ards and were duly castigated for actions over which they could have had no control.

Part of the conceptual competence required from boards is to consider the very long-term (i.e. 25 or so years) implications of their organisation's actions and, while this may have been almost impossible in the past, current and emerging technology makes this not only possible today, but essential.

With so many companies globally collapsing due to ethical issues, it is clear that one of the board's roles is to govern the ethical system. However, if the focus is always on the governance side, how will the organisation move forward and improve? To do so, boards must direct the organisation on how to become ethical and how to gain strategic advantage and future value from its ethical business operations.

Peter Tunjic[24] separates governance and directorship into two distinct systems of thoughts and actions within the one boardroom. Governance is focused on determining the correct structure and process for preserving value through controls and risk management. Directorship involves mak-ing decisions that, by default, create some risks and leading from the top. He claims that most boards are too focused on compliance and measuring the cash value (governance) and, in doing so, are ignoring their roles in creating value (directorship). Directorship is important for board mem-bers. Many of them see strategy as the most vital issue but, in their article about where boards fall short, Barton and Wiseman[25] refer to McKinsey research in 2014 which found that a majority of directors do not believe that they fully comprehend their company's strategy.

This is because the current corporate governance system is not designed to create value. The best practice today still focuses too nar-rowly on governance and protecting value and not enough on creating it. Peter Tunjic takes his argument one step further and connects ethics not to the governance role, but to that of directorship, which he calls value creation. Yes, you heard us right, ethics creates value for the organisa-tion! And it is the board that needs not only to govern and control what is going on in the organisation ethically, but also to explicitly lead the organisation ethically. Leading ethically means demonstrating transpar-ency in both the governance and directorship roles of the board. In his words, Tunjic says, 'directing for value requires that the board does the right things. Governing for value protection is about doing things right.'

Another aspect of the corporate governance system today is that it is structured to work for the benefit of the company's shareholders without concerning itself with the future of the surrounding environment and communities. This puts the board in an inherent ethical conflict. On the one hand, they exist to govern and direct the company in the interests of the shareholders. On the other hand, the shareholders' interests are often short term and the organisation needs to survive in the long term. And what should they do in a case when protecting one set of shareholders' interests can cause damage to others?

Another pressure on boards to prefer short-termism over the long-term sustainability of the organisation is the financial markets. Many boards overemphasise the short term to justify the current organisational success. However, the fiduciary duty of directors means that they should do their best to ensure that the organisation thrives for many years ahead, rather than focus mainly on short-term financial performance. Their focus should be on wealth maximisation rather than on profit maximisation.

The issue of social media

Social media has a huge impact on the workplace today and presents a whole range of ethical issues, such as bullying, intimidation, etc. But it also has a huge impact in terms of disruptive practices. Consider the impact of the rise of services such as Uber[26] on the traditional taxi business model. In Australia, taxi licence owners who paid extremely large amounts for their right to provide the service now face significant ongoing costs in relation to passenger bookings. Insurance and training providers, etc. suddenly find themselves undercut by a service that has few, if any, of their overheads and which utilises social media to the full. Another example is the rise of Airbnb. Using social media to promote this concept has had a significant impact on the traditional accommodation market. Around the world, individuals, coordinated through a central agency, can offer rooms in their homes at a rate far lower than traditional hotels and motels. This is challenging traditional models across much of the travel and tourism industry because the new entrants face few if any of the overheads and regulations impacting traditional providers.

The legal environment

On 31 March 2016, the international media reported evidence of was vast corruption in the oil industry.[27] The claim was that a Monaco-based company, Unaoil, had been involved in unethical behaviour in the years 2002 to 2012 and that internationally known household names, such as Rolls-Royce, Halliburton, Leighton Holdings, Samsung and Hyundai, were all implicated. Only a few days later, the same media were disclosing another scandal concerning the magnitude of profit shifting and tax avoidance that was being undertaken across the world. This second report was based on an investigation of some 11.5 million leaked financial and legal records covering a 40-year period and involving an investigating team comprising more than 370 journalists across 76 countries. This investigation, now known as the 'Panama Papers' and led by the International Consortium of Investigative Journalists,[28] argued that politicians, business leaders and criminals were among a large group of people and organisations that used the services of a Panama-based law firm, Mossack Fonseca, to move money and assets through complicated networks of companies and trusts, into jurisdictions in which little or no tax was paid. They made it clear that a key part of Mossack and Fonesca's services entailed ensuring that the task of regulatory and investigative bodies was made as difficult as possible – and, ideally, that the money was impossible to trace. A key difference between the Unaoil and the Panama Papers stories was that, in the case of the Panama Papers, it was not alleged or implied that Mossack and Fonesca had broken any laws.

One of the courses that Douglas teaches at the University of New South Wales requires students to consider such cases as whistleblowing in the Commonwealth Bank,[29] offshore outsourcing in the clothing industry[30] and the Rana Plaza disaster in Bangladesh.[31] In each of these, students consider the relationship between doing what is legal and doing what is moral or ethical. Clearly, in some of these cases the activities are neither legal nor ethical but it is interesting to see students grapple with this issue in a post facto manner. Given the subject matter and the presentations of these issues through the media, the students generally have little difficulty in identifying both the legal and the ethical issues, but when this is extrapolated to other stories that may be found in the current daily media relating to business strategy they are usually far less clear regarding the legal versus ethical issue – especially when confronted with both the concepts of overall business strategy in a globalised society and the Panama Papers.

And, in part, it is the globalised society which has been a key influence in corporate unethical behaviour.

In his book *The Collapse of Globalism*,[32] John Ralston Saul traces the rise of globalism and provides a commentary on its strengths and weaknesses. One of the points he makes (p. 29) is that US President

George Bush Senior, in promoting globalism, introduced the phrase 'free markets and free men' into one of his speeches even though history shows that it is actually free men that produce free markets rather than the reverse. Saul goes on to provide many examples of the ways in which globalism operates and it quickly becomes clear that the emphasis has moved to accentuating the legality of actions rather than either the morality per se or, alternatively, the combined legality and morality. As the book develops, it appears as though this movement away from consideration of the morality of action is seen by Saul as one of the reasons why he believes that, eventually, nations will revert to some form of protectionism in order to maintain national identity and national culture. (As an aside, perhaps this is already being seen in the Brexit movement's success in the recent referendum, in which a slim majority of UK voters determined that Britain should leave the European Union.) Understandably, of course, any move that has the potential to weaken or reduce the opportunity for wealthy nations to exploit more vulnerable nations – something that has clearly happened under globalisation – will be strenuously opposed and the proponents punished. Despite this, there appears to be some external support for Saul's premise, given that the economic law of diminishing returns demonstrates that it is becoming increasingly difficult to maintain economic growth at the levels attained over the past 40 or so years because resources in developing countries are becoming increasingly scarce and countries appear to be increasingly concerned to preserve those resources that they still control. Of course, given the recent exposure of unethical conduct across the world, it appears as though this reduction in available resources which are capable of easy exploitation has itself also caused organisations and individuals to focus on what is legal rather than on what is ethical.

The philosopher John Rawls[33] talks of the need for justice as a key component of ethical behaviour. Building on the work of such philosophy luminaries as Immanuel Kant and David Hume, he argues that justice should guide behaviour and that when it is not obviously guiding behaviour, we have unethical activity. In relation to economic ethics, Rawls argues that any imbalance of justice should be skewed towards the least advantaged of society rather than, as is the case at present, towards the most advantaged of society. He sees justice as equating with fairness and unethical behaviour as anything that is not demonstrably fair to all parties. In other words, he argues for an egalitarian society in which there is a genuine concern for the disadvantaged and a correspondingly genuine desire to narrow the inequality gap. He suggests that, in deciding whether or not a proposed course of action is ethical, we should use the hypothetical concept of designing a 'good' or 'just' society. Only if our proposed action would help to promulgate a 'good' or 'just' society can it be judged to be ethical.

Unethical or corrupt?

In July 2008, the Academy of Management published several studies dealing with corruption in both individuals and organisations.[34] One article[35] makes the point that corruption is found everywhere, in all types of organisations, and goes on to observe that 'an inordinate number of organizations, along with their leaders and their agents, appear to have failed the most elementary of all ethics tests'. In other words, the article implies that there is a link between ethics and corruption. The same article also states that 'the notion of corrupt behaviour overlaps somewhat with related notions in the management literature, including unethical behaviour'. The authors then go on to describe corruption as 'moral deterioration' and imply that unethical behaviour is also indicative of moral deterioration, as are all negative organisational behaviours in general. While such behaviours are not necessarily corruption per se, the authors see these as creating 'a crucible for corruption'.

Linking unethical behaviour with corrupt behaviour may seem extreme and, for some people, offensive. However, the *Oxford Dictionary* describes corruption as, inter alia, 'untrustworthy' and surely, if a person or organisation cannot be trusted to behave in an ethical manner, then that person or organisation is 'untrustworthy' and there exists, therefore, at least the seeds of corruption. And this is the point made in the *Academy of Management Review* paper – 'a crucible for corruption' has developed. It develops, since the boundaries between ethical and unethical behaviour become blurred when unethical practices are not addressed (are either accepted or ignored), so that they become part of the organisational culture. As the boundaries between right and wrong are eroded within the culture, the door opens to corruption. In such cultures, it is difficult to observe the corruption. Often, even when employees are aware that something is going badly wrong, they will not draw any attention to it because this has become 'the way we do things around here'.

Further light is shed on this 'crucible for corruption' in the work of David Eagleman. In a television series on how our brain works[36] Eagleman states that 'the "real world" is an illusion constructed in your head' and goes on to illustrate that, once our brains become accustomed to particular patterns, they will 'see' those patterns even though the reality may be quite different. He shows that we see what we expect to see and that our past experience has developed within us a set of conditions through which we interpret every incoming stimulus. Although Eagleman does not discuss ethical versus unethical behaviour, the logic flowing from his study indicates that it must follow that, if our brains become accustomed to a pattern of behaviour that third parties consider to be unethical, then there is a high probability that eventually we may totally lose our facility to distinguish between ethical and unethical behaviour until, eventually, unethical behaviour degenerates into corrupt behaviour.

Perhaps this 'seeing what we expect to see' is a factor in the apparent inability of some company directors to recognise unethical behaviour in their organisations. Ashforth et al. in the previously mentioned *Academy of Management Review* paper suggest that if the norms and practices (i.e. the culture) of an organisation operate

> mainly to serve the competitive interests of a company in the unbridled drive for profits at any cost, they run the risk of shouldering aside other norms that might serve the interests of other stakeholders, including those of the larger society.

Is this what happened at James Hardie Industries and their response to asbestos problems? More recently, given the exposure of questionable ethical practices in the insurance industry in Australia[37] with particular reference to Comminsure or to the behaviour of financial planners and others in the Australian banking industry, is it that those at the top (i.e. the board) are actually highly ethical people who simply see what they expect to see rather than what is actually the case?

There are no simple answers to these questions but they do highlight the need for company directors to be actively moving around the organisations for which they are responsible to see for themselves what is happening and to question their observations in regard to their personal assumptions. In the military it is commonplace to teach service men and women that, when operating 'in the field', in order to minimise the risk of missing anything important, observations should be done in a manner that is the exact opposite of our normal way of scanning. Our normal way of looking at scenery (at least in the Western world) is to move from left to right and from top to bottom. Service people are taught to scan their environment from right to left and from bottom to top – that way anything different from what one expected to see is more likely to become apparent. Of course, no matter which means of observation is used, the important thing is that observation actually occurs – and that, unfortunately, is something that, all too often, is not done by company directors, many of whom seem to believe that their only role is to read reports and to attend and participate in board meetings.

Regulators work in a politically sensitive environment. They are looking at past events and only after significant affairs do they craft new regulations. The process of regulating is very long and hence the response to these events can take years to implement. Regulation needs to anticipate if it is to be effective. Moreover, regulation addresses systems and processes, yet behaviours are also cultural in nature.

Over the years, changes in the legislation covering directors' liability have made the governance role more complex. Until quite recently, boards expected their management teams to deal with issues such as ethics and culture. In many cases, relevant discussions had already taken place in the boardrooms of manufacturing organisations (especially in relation to occupational health and safety). However, in finance and services organisations, ethics and culture issues didn't necessarily reach the boardroom prior to the introduction of more complex directors' liability.

To quote one interviewee, as the legal environment strengthens the rules relating to governance, compliance comes 'front and center. This makes the ethical debate disappear'. These regulations 'created a compliance culture. "Is it legal?" We have gone so far with regulation that it seems we have created the notion that if we are compliant, it means that we are OK. But this is not the case'. Compliance is not necessarily the same as doing the right thing. To quote several interviewed chairs:

> Often, the legal is below what's right to do. Legally we can do it, but is it the right thing to do?
> With the societal changes, our customers are looking for the companies to act ethically and do the right thing.
> Giving value for customers, not just leading a good business ... You shouldn't rip people off.

The combination of rapid societal change and limited governance change presents further challenges for board members. Many have mentioned similar concerns, that 'people are now judged for something they have done in the past, using today's standards'.

Inherent ethical issues in corporate governance vs society's expectations

Today's governance system is predicated on organisations with scarce resources (such as time and money) that are managed by people who might build and use their power inappropriately and unethically in relation to society at large. The relationships between organisations and society are complex. On the one hand, consumers globally are demanding lower costs and, on the other hand, to achieve these costs, organisations look for solutions in the wider society. In recent years we have seen increasing numbers of people and groups that are worried about this issue.

The integral trade framework, developed by David Martin and mentioned in Chapter 3, asserts that when people are informed correctly, they will choose according to what is right and decline products that were developed by exploitation of the environment or a certain community/society. In other words, it assumes that what organisations see as ethical means to accommodate consumers' cravings for lower prices, can actually be perceived by the consumers themselves as unethical. For example, Martin's premise is that, if people knew that a certain product was cheap due to slavery, they would have accepted paying a higher cost in order to alleviate working conditions that can be equated with slavery.

Withholding information from consumers can be perceived as an unethical behaviour in itself and hence transparency is needed to allow society to govern the ethical operation of organisations. Boards are then in a position where, in order to ensure the long-term sustainability of the organisation, they must direct ethical behaviours throughout the organisational operations.

So, now let us consider the situation in the organisations we studied.

Notes

1 See http://knowledge.wharton.upenn.edu/special-report/special-report-on-business-ethics-enhancing-corporate-governance/?utm_source=kw_newsletter&utm_medium=email&utm_campaign=2016-02-25 [21 July 2016].
2 See https://www.youtube.com/watch?v=sD67LKqXGrg [22 July 2016].
3 See the analysis of Graves' pioneering work in Beck, D. and Cowan, C. (1996) *Spiral Dynamics: Mastering Values, Leadership and Change*, Blackwell, USA.
4 Beck and Cowan (1996) op. cit.
5 Adonis, J. (2015) 'Do corporate values matter?', *Canberra Times*, 4 September.
6 Guiso, L., Sapienza, P. and Zingales, L. (2015) *Journal of Financial Economics*, Vol. 117, Issue 1, July, pp. 60–76.
7 Long, D. G. (2013) *Delivering High Performance: The Third Generation Organisation*, Gower, UK.
8 Beck and Cowan (1996) op. cit.
9 See http://www.abc.net.au/foreign/content/2011/s3359246.htm [22 July 2016]. Originally broadcast in Australia 8 November 2011.
10 This concept is largely based on the work of Milton Friedman (Friedman, M. (1962) *Capitalism and Freedom*, Phoenix Books, Chicago).
11 See http://www.canberratimes.com.au/business/banking-and-finance/the-search-for-the-perfect-company-20151021-gkeocv [22 July 2016].
12 Tomlinson, C. (2015) The truth about corporate ethics is still out there, *New York Times*, reported in the *Sydney Morning Herald*, Friday 9 October (p. 28).
13 Sir John Harvey-Jones, *The Company Chairman* (as quoted in Long, D. G. (2012) *Third Generation Leadership and the Locus of Control*, Gower, London).

14 Shields, J., O'Donnell, M. and O'Brien, J. (2003) *The Bucks Stop Here: Private Sector Executive Remuneration in Australia*. Report prepared for the Labor Council of New South Wales.

15 See http://www.smh.com.au/business/the-motivation-myth-and-why-government-incentives-result-in-greedy-behaviour-20151224-glun6t.html [22 July 2016].

16 Jaques, E. (1998) *Requisite Organisation: A Total System for Effective Managerial Organization and Managerial Leadership for the 21st Century*, Cason Hall & Co, Arlington, VA, USA.

17 See http://knowledge.wharton.upenn.edu/article/the-power-of-treating-employees-like-family/?utm_source=kw_newsletter&utm_medium=email&utm_campaign=2015-11-06 [22 July 2016].

18 Some of this story is discussed by Allan Moyes in *Quality Leadership: A Group of Essays* (1997), CLS, Sydney.

19 Her actual statement was 'There is no such thing as society. There are individuals, and there are families'.

20 See http://www.smh.com.au/business/ceo-pay-more-complicated-than-it-looks-20150112-12mg19.html [25 July 2016].

21 Friedman, M. (1962) *Capitalism and Freedom*, Phoenix Books, Chicago.

22 See http://www.forbes.com/sites/stevedenning/2013/06/26/the-origin-of-the-worlds-dumbest-idea-milton-friedman/ [25 July 2016].

23 See http://www.smh.com.au/business/the-economy/these-20-americans-own-more-wealth-than-half-the-us-population-combined-20151207-glha3i.html [25 July 2016].

24 *Governance*, October 2013, Issue 233, p. 8.

25 See https://hbr.org/2015/01/where-boards-fall-short [25 July 2016].

26 See http://www.canberratimes.com.au/act-news/the-man-with-most-to-lose-if-uber-makes-major-inroads-into-canberras-taxi-business-20151201-glcg5i.html [25 July 2016].

27 See http://www.theage.com.au/interactive/2016/the-bribe-factory/day-1/the-company-that-bribed-the-world.html [25 July 2016].

28 See https://panamapapers.icij.org/ [25 July 2016].

29 See http://www.abc.net.au/4corners/stories/2016/03/07/4417757.htm [25 July 2016].

30 See http://www.smh.com.au/business/surf-clothing-label-rip-curl-using-slave-labour-to-manufacture-clothes-in-north-korea-20160219-gmz375.html#ixzz40kLo7xkl [25 July 2016].

31 See http://www.abc.net.au/4corners/stories/2013/06/25/3785918.htm [25 July 2016].

32 Saul, J. R. (2005) *The Collapse of Globalism and the Reinvention of the World*, Penguin, Camberwell, Victoria, Australia.

33 Rawls, J. (1971) *A Theory of Justice*, Belknap Press, Harvard University, Cambridge, MA.

34 *Academy of Management Review*, Vol. 33, No. 3, July, 2008.

35 Ashforth, B. E., Gioia, D. A., Robinson, S. L., Treviño, L. K. (2008) Re-viewing organizational corruption, *Academy of Management Review*, Vol. 33, No. 3, July, pp. 670–684.

36 See http://www.pbs.org/show/brain-david-eagleman/ [10 August 2016].

37 Previously available at http://iview.abc.net.au/programs/four-corners/NC1604H006S00 [7 March 2016].

6   The ethics kaleidoscope: gaining strategic advantage

As described in previous chapters, the environment within which boards and organisations operate is full of ethical challenges. The day-to-day activities also present major ethical issues for boards to resolve. However, interestingly, our research revealed that most chairs and directors described ethical issues from a single point of reference. They focus their ethical attention on a certain type of risk at the board or the organisational levels. While doing so, they rarely consider other areas in which ethics is critical. Taking all the areas of concern suggested by our interviewees, we would like to suggest a different way of looking at ethics.

Ethics in the boardroom and in the organisation can be considered in many ways, or through many different lenses. Each one of them creates opportunities and helps to govern risks. By constantly reviewing each of these lenses, the ethics kaleidoscope provides a different picture that leads to a strategic advantage.

In order to gain strategic advantage, board involvement is crucial. Some chairs and board members admitted that, in the main, ethical issues come up only when they are raised by the management team. This statement carries risks, as the boards in these companies trust their management teams blindly. Ethics should be discussed at board level and should be owned by the board. Consider the global companies that have collapsed in recent years – in the main they foundered because of ethical issues. We do not suggest that boards should distrust their management teams as a default stance; however, there should be an understanding that management reports can, consciously or unconsciously, be biased.

Often, ethical issues are brought to the board's attention only after something has gone wrong. In these cases, it is too late and the board's attention is then focused on damage control. While aware of ethics and its importance, many interviewees reported that once ethical issues were brought to the board level, it 'shocked us, rocked us!' This is due to the absence of mindfulness. Directors are not considering ethics until it is too late. The ethics kaleidoscope framework allows you to proactively manage by considering the different lenses.

Ethical issues are often hidden and hard to read, especially when the board meets once a month. We have seen examples of boards that are trying to avoid taking the blame. Others admit responsibility, but claim that they could not have known about ethical issues. The ethics kaleidoscope provides a new framework to open boards' awareness to ethics, a vitally important area, as discussed in Chapter 2 on the connection between ethics and the Johari Window.

In order to elevate the ethical risk into a strategic advantage, the different lenses should be considered by all boards, regardless of industry, purpose or structure.

Next, we will introduce each of the lenses (see Figure 2). However, before explaining them, we would like to emphasise that ethics is a function of directorship. Boards are groups of people with a wide diversity of thoughts. Having people with different backgrounds, knowledge and expertise allows boards to look at situations thoroughly and from many different angles. The same applies to managing ethics. The beauty of boards is that each director brings her or his own view, looking via the same lens. The diversity of views and robust discussions are key to success in managing ethics.

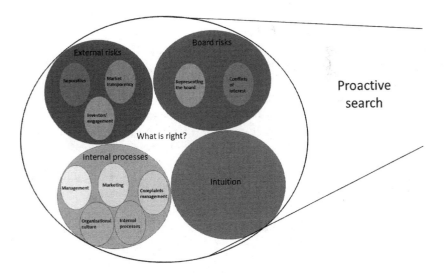

Figure 2 The lenses of the ethics kaleidoscope

Lens 1: External risks

Reputational risk

This lens looks at ethics as a risk factor that, when not managed well, can potentially severely damage the organisational reputation. One of the interviewees explained this lens in the following terms:

> I have an atheist view of ethics, it's all about the risks. Do I care about having GMO wheat in my food? NO, but I raise it at the board meeting because it's a big issue in the media. I am interested in the risk mitigation point of view, not if it is healthy or not.

Reputation is very hard to build but you can blow it up with one unethical decision. You only have one reputation. The easiest way to lose it is to behave unethically.

The reputational risk extends beyond the operation of the specific organisation to its entire supply chain. Companies are now at risk of reputational damage when choosing suppliers and contractors. The fashion industry is one example of Western companies needing to defend their reputation after revealing the nature of employment at their suppliers' sites (with issues such as employment of children, slavery conditions, low salaries, etc.).

Market transparency and disclosure

This is one of the biggest dilemmas which boards of public companies face. On the one hand, there is a need to keep the market and investors informed; on the other hand, often confidentiality is required for successful strategy implementation.

- When is the appropriate time to inform the market about a new strategy? If you release the information too early, it can bump up the shares price and at the same time allow competitors to respond earlier.
- When is it appropriate not to release information? There have been many cases of companies that chose not to disclose information that could have affected their share price.
- Do you keep shareholders and investors informed according to the legal requirements or because you see it as important?

The above questions were raised by chairpersons of public companies, but can be applied to NFPs as well, since many NFPs are involved in fundraising and/or receive government funding. Reporting on responsible money management and how they utilise the donated or granted money to further their cause is key for NFPs' long-term sustainability.

Investors' engagement

The global environment is changing rapidly. Investors are now taking a view of what is right, taking account of the environment, wider society and religious aspects. These investors are influenced by different pressure/lobbying groups in the market. The stronger the pressure group is, the more likely it is that investors will be influenced, even in cases where the pressure group intends to damage the company's reputation.

- Some board members hold the opinion that ethics means remembering that the board represents all the investors, regardless of the size of their stockholding.
- Companies also face lobbying groups with competing agendas. When working with these groups, we need to remember that every ethical dilemma has, at least, two sides. For example, do you invest in a company which has a mining operation in an African country that has poor human rights? On the other hand, this company provides work for poor people. How do you weigh the factors in the balance?
- How do you identify the relevant groups and to what degree should you change your strategy based on your analysis?
- A few interviewees raised concerns about investors and shareholders who tried to actively undermine the company in order to reduce its value.

Lens 2: Internal processes

Using this lens, boards are encouraged to look into the internal processes within the organisation: management, marketing, supply chain, procurement, complaint management and other internal processes. While these are led by the top and middle management on a day-to-day basis, they are based on ethical assumptions, decisions and practices. Each one of these processes is crucial to organisational success and can provide a strategic advantage, but only if carried out in an ethical manner.

Management

As discussed in the first part of the book, it is the leadership behaviour that matters and sets the ethical tone in the organisation. Who constitutes the leadership? Some would say the board, others would argue the top management. We believe that it is the dynamic between the board and the top management that sets the ethical tone.

What licence do boards give CEOs and the top management team in terms of behaviour? Boards are liable for the physical and mental health of their employees. This responsibility begins at the top, in fact, from the board table to the CEO and other executives. It then penetrates down to the team. The same applies to telling the truth. We don't need to train employees not to tell a lie. However, if they see managers and executives lying, they think it is acceptable in the organisation. After all, this behaviour got those individuals where they are now and they keep on getting promoted. Here we would like to remind you of the example of Orica, mentioned in Chapter 3. The company's financial results were good but the board decided that the CEO's behaviour was unacceptable. Allowing the CEO's unethical behaviour to continue unchecked means providing a licence for everyone else in the organisation to behave in the same way.

Another aspect for boards to bear in mind and monitor is the integrity of reporting. Although, generally, management should be trusted, behind every report are hidden conscious and/or unconscious agendas and perceptions of the situation. Reports are built in a certain way and there is a process of decision making behind the information that is included in or excluded from the report. Questioning and understanding the logic behind the report building provides a way for boards to examine the management ethics.

Boards impose both implicit and explicit expectations on the top management. Often managers feel under pressure to deliver under any circumstances. Unfortunately, there are some examples of executives who lied to the board because they were afraid that they might lose their job if they told the truth. Boards must ensure that they create an atmosphere that encourages executives and employees to raise ethical concerns without fear of reprisal. This atmosphere is key to success.

Complaints management

Complaints from shareholders, customers, stakeholders and employees can reveal deeper ethical issues. The process by which they are collected, managed, analysed and reported should be of great interest to boards and can lead to important insights.

Actively looking at complaint management means:

1   encouraging the top management to develop a proactive complaint resolution approach and looking at complaints as 'gifts' that eventually lead to opportunities for change and strategic advantage;

2   realising that reporting is a biased tool – boards must question the logic behind the report building and which complaints are included and determine the rationale behind excluding certain complaints;

3   looking for common denominators between complaints that, on the surface, do not appear to be related to one another. Is there a hidden ethical similarity linking them all?

Marketing

Marketing is an important function that helps the organisation in creating and delivering value to customers and in managing customer relationships to the benefit of the company and its shareholders. An organisation that cannot satisfy its customers will not survive. For this purpose, marketing is focused on researching and understanding the customers' needs and what will satisfy them. Marketing then translates this knowledge into exchange relationships – the customers receive something they value and the company translates the exchange into profit. While all this sounds very simple and logical, it is not necessarily so in practice. If this really were the case, why did so many chairpersons raise ethical dilemmas that are related to marketing?

The ongoing study of market needs and consumer behaviour is essential for most organisations. This study should, of course, be conducted in an ethical manner and the board must ensure ethical conduct. However, most chairs are actually worried about the secondary function of marketing – creating, communicating and delivering to customers. Ethical dilemmas about marketing misrepresentations have been raised in many of our interviews. Marketing is, essentially, sending positive messages to the right audience. How accurate is the marketing of any given certain product? This is a matter for ethical determination. Some useful examples can be gleaned from the medicine and cosmetics industry. In terms of the research that companies share with consumers – do they advertise results of clinical experiments that failed or only those that succeeded? Do they represent the product's advantages accurately? What information has been excluded from advertising? It is the board's role to define the ethical boundaries of marketing and ensure the product or service on offer is represented truthfully.

Procurement

Another area to which the board needs to devote attention and where it must clearly define its expectations is procurement and its probity. Procurement (both nationally and globally) can attract fraud.

One example out of many is the false invoicing uncovered at the Department of Education and Training, Victoria, in 2015.[1] When people are involved in acts such as false invoicing, cartels in procurement and other practices, they know that they are involved in illegal activity. Hence, they plan their actions and hide them well.

However, the discussion about procurement and ethics goes beyond the letter of the law. Probity and ethics deal with what is right and fair. They call for equitable treatment of all parties and transparent and accountable processes throughout the entire procurement process. Any procurement process should be guided by consistent ethical behaviour: honesty, integrity and fairness. It is the board's role to set the direction and expectations for ethical procurement, as well as to ensure that these guidelines are followed.

Supply chain

While procurement deals with decisions made inside the organisation, what happens in the operations throughout the supply chain widens the ethical dilemmas beyond the organisation's decisions zone, yet keeps its accountability in place. *Behind the Barcode*, a report by Baptist World Aid Australia,[2] finds that in the fashion industry about half of the companies have fully traced their supply chains back to their final manufacturers, but only 9 per cent have fully traced back to the raw materials. Only 14 per cent are ensuring that their contractors are paying some form of living wage and only 10 per cent regularly conduct unannounced audits. Occupational health and safety issues throughout the supply chain are another area of concern.

The 2013 collapse of the Rana Plaza building in Bangladesh[3] caused a death toll of 1,129 and approximately 2,515 injured people were rescued. The building contained a clothing factory, a bank, apartments and shops. When cracks were discovered in the building, the shops and the bank immediately closed. However, the garment employees were ordered to return to work. Another example is when Apple's subcontractors' assembly plants in China[4] were found to be using safety nets around the various levels of their buildings to prevent workers from committing suicide. Suicide is not a culturally normative act in China, but it was, for some people, the only possible response to the employment conditions these employees were facing.

The issue of ethical behaviour throughout the supply chain is strongly related to the social dilemma described in Chapter 5 on the macro perspective. Consumers' demand for lower costs and distribution of products all year round results in organisations trying to lower the costs of their supply chain. However, at the same time, society is expecting organisations to maintain integrity and act ethically. Consumers do not wish lower costs to equate with exploitation of communities, people and the environment.

Tracing ethical management throughout the supply chain is not an easy task. Many organisations struggle to achieve full accountability and the supply chain can be very long, making this effort a resource-intensive task. However, the risk of ignoring this task is high and it is worthwhile investing the necessary effort.

Other internal processes for boards' attention

What is considered to be an ethical practice and how long does it take for unethical issues to be raised at board level are two questions that were mentioned by many interviewees. The answer to both question is simple: it takes too long and often it is too late before ethical issues are discussed at board level and it is not always clear cut what the board considers to be unethical practice.

In large organisations (public and private), ethical issues sometimes only reach board level after some two years have passed. 'We don't know about the breaches until a campaign is built.' When they are finally raised at board level, it is often too late and the board's role then is focused on damage control. The board must ensure that the internal processes are defined in a way that will allow ethical issues to be brought to its attention on a regular basis and not only after they have escalated into a crisis.

NFPs are often perceived as more ethical than for-profit organisations that are focused on creating monetary value for their shareholders. However, further to the discussion in the first part of the book, some NFPs seem to suffer from a lack of good infrastructure for money management – with flawed accounting practices, rolling money from one year to another without reporting to grant providers and missing money in financial records being common examples. Federal and State money is provided to NFPs, yet evidence indicates that only about 25 per cent of this money actually goes towards the cause itself. The rest is spent on administration. The purpose of grant money is not to keep the NFP afloat, but it is to be utilised in supporting the cause. Allowing 75 per cent of this money to be channelled into salaries and other administrative costs was mentioned by a few interviewees as a common unethical practice in the NFP sector.

Lens 3: Board risks

In the second lens we described ethical leadership as the dynamic between board and management and encouraged boards to keep the behaviour of the top management under constant review. This lens actually deals with the board proactively evaluating its own ethical operation. The board is composed of executive and non-executive directors. Some directors are independent while others represent shareholders. Each, individually, may have different ethical standards and different agendas. As a group, they set the ethical tone of the organisation. This complexity involves some ethical questions that need to be evaluated by the board on a regular basis.

Conflict of interest

In many cases we have heard stories about directors who don't declare their conflicts of interest or who declare them, but work behind the scenes (outside the voting discussion) with their fellow directors to ensure that any resolution is in their interest. In one case, a director refused to leave the boardroom while a discussion about an issue in which he had a personal interest was taking place. The message for the directors was clear – although I cannot vote, I do hear and see your choices. In another example, a board member tried to force his colleagues into a resolution to appoint him personally to provide a paid service to the organisation. When resistance was raised, he did all he could to try to remove those directors who opposed him from the board.

We would like to extend the definition of conflict of interest to any behaviour of a director or chairperson that puts his or her agenda before that of the company. When directors are also investors or representatives of investors, they may find themselves thinking about their own interests, rather than those of the company. Often these interests focus on short-term profit, rather than the long-term survival of the organisation. In our research, we found that directors of large companies are often more careful in terms of policing possible conflicts of interest than those in small or medium-sized private or NFP companies. Regardless of the size and purpose of the organisation, we need to remember that the ethics of the company is the ethics of the people who lead it.

Representing the board

The board's decisions are comprised of the decisions of each individual member. Once the board has made a decision, it is expected that each of its members will stand behind that decision (no matter whether the director voted for or against the decision). This is the standard expected from every manager as well.

However, on interviewee raised the question 'What do you do when the board makes a decision you voted against, because it is not ethical in your view? What do you do? It's a higher level than a financial problem.' Each of the board members needs to feel confident with the board's decisions. A couple of chairpersons suggested that this situation should be an indication of when it's time to move on and resign from the board. They argue that if a decision is perceived by the individual as unethical and after raising the issue with the board it seems that there is an ethical gap, it is time to resign and contribute to other companies. After all, our ethics is our guiding compass.

Lens 4: Organisational culture

As we discussed in the previous chapters, organisational culture and ethics are strongly embedded one in another. Ethics is part of the culture's DNA. It is very difficult for board members to have a true feel for the company's culture and how supportive of ethics it is. However, ethical problems are like a virus in the company – once they take root, they are highly contagious. Hence, boards must pay close attention to ethics.

Transparency

Being distanced from the organisation, it is hard for board members to actually know what the organisational culture is in practice. Too often there is a loose connection between the stated organisational values and the actual practices. In order to understand the true culture of the organisation, the board needs to create a culture of transparency. This will allow managers to say what they want to say and raise ethical concerns, as well as encouraging transparency throughout the organisation. Again, to quote chairpersons:

> It's not feasible within 12 meetings a year to really know what's going on. You can do internal audit or use external consultants. But this doesn't replace the trust and reliance on management and CEO.
> You've got to trust the management. Board members cannot know the culture. You can sense and smell, but don't have empirical data.

This transparency is crucial to enable boards to evaluate the health of the organisational culture. In our research, chairs indicated a few disruptive cultures that are hard to identify.

Disruptive cultures

Many interviewees provided examples of organisational and boardroom cultures that were disruptive for governance and prevented achievement of goals and success, some of which are detailed below.

A culture of cover-up

When the organisation has a culture of management covering up problems it takes time for the board to learn about issues, especially ethical ones. This type of culture typically involves blaming, lying and reporting on events only after attempting to fix them. A cover-up culture is actually easier to identify than people think. Taking accountability rather than blaming others and fully reporting on issues on time is the basis of the desired culture. If this is not the case, the board needs to take an active role in changing the culture. An accountable culture comes from the top.

An immune culture

An immune culture can develop in the boardroom or at the top management table, and sometimes in both. This type of culture is built from years of experience that cause decision makers to become immune to complaints, conflicts and other challenges. It is the common notion of 'that's normal, nothing is perfect'. 'You become immune to a certain customer dissatisfaction level' and then when it becomes the board's culture, the entrenched group thinking prevents an efficient governance from developing.

Self-serving agendas

When people put their personal gain ahead of doing the right thing by the organisation and this behavior is tolerated, it can easily become part of the organisational culture. When it percolates down through the ranks, ethical issues start arising at many levels. The longer it goes on, the deeper it penetrates into internal organisational processes. At this stage, only a major transformation would help, as it is no longer an individual problem, but becomes an inherent cultural and operational practice.

It is therefore imperative for boards to create a transparent culture and ensure that the organisational culture is not just something 'fluffy' that management reports on in general terms, but an area where each of the board members feels confident in their leadership role.

Lens 5: Intuition

One of the interesting points that was raised by several interviewees is that, in many cases, they had an intuition that something was wrong yet felt that, as board members, they could not act solely upon their gut feelings; they needed hard data to prove they were right. In the end, their intuition was correct, but it took a long time to find actual evidence of unethical behaviours that they could act upon. By the time the evidence was gathered (one or two years later) severe damage had already been done to the organisation.

One of the many examples from our interviews:

> I caught the CEO lying. It took me two years to expose him. No one else in the board supported me. I could never get a straight-forward answer from him and every part of my intuition indicated that he is lying. But the other directors said 'he is such a nice guy, what's your problem?' You can't do anything based on intuition only, so I forced a restructure that included promotion of a few top executives. Those who have complied with him so far and didn't disclose to the board what is really going on, all of a sudden had responsibilities and started talking about all the breaches that happened there behind the board's back … Every part of me indicated 'he is lying'. But I couldn't do anything drastic based on intuition only.

Many other interviewees shared examples of when their intuition screamed 'Danger! Something is wrong.' The common themes were:

- Board members and executives that don't like to be asked about their arguments and point of views. Some of them become aggressive, others ignore questions or constantly manoeuvre discussions when they are asked difficult questions.
- Board members and executives that repeatedly raise issues of interest to the group in one-on-one meetings only, rather than addressing the problems with the board or management team in an open manner.
- Executives that repeatedly provide more information than the board can cope with or too little information, which keeps the topic vague, or communicate information around the topic without getting to the main issues.
- Covering up bad news. How soon does the board hear about bad news? 'Makes me nervous when bad news drives slowly, when people are trying to fix the problem before they tell you about it.'
- Constant delays in supplying board papers and regular last-minute changes.
- Body language – looking at the behaviours around the table. Specifically mentioned was body language that contradicts the verbal message and signs of nervousness during certain discussions.

At the board there is a collective wisdom. Harness intuition as part of this wisdom.

What is right?

Ethics can be viewed as risk management – not the response to risk, but the way you manage risks. It is a combination of taking a wide lens approach together with minimising risks and issues by dealing with them ethically. Hence, the middle lens that should be used in combination with each of these lenses is the important question of what is the right thing to do? There is a long-term cost for doing the wrong thing. The right decision is often beyond what is defined by the law. It requires thinking about employees, investors, shareholders, stakeholders, suppliers, society as a whole and the environment. You can follow the letter of the law, but still be unethical. The importance of being ethical and adopting a holistic approach is key to gaining a sustainable strategic advantage.

A proactive search

In order to gain strategic advantage from managing ethics, the board must add ethics to its agenda and proactively review each of the lenses. If you just deal with ethical issues when they arise, the organisation will not survive. Ethics is the solution, not the dilemma.

> The idea that boards should wait until ethical issues arise is ridiculous. It's like waiting for the disease to become cancer stage 4. It's too late. Needs to treat at level 1 or pre-cancer.
> The role of the board is to smell the smoke. If you wait until you can see the ethical issue, it's too late.

Ethics is about being forward-looking, not about focusing on apportioning blame for what has already happened. There is ethics in every decision you need to take. Actively bring ethics to the table as part of the decision making.

An important note to explain the kaleidoscope: how board members construct knowledge

The beauty of the ethics kaleidoscope is in its acknowledgement that, by looking through different lenses, we see a different perspective of the organisational ethics system. However, it is important to note that different people looking through the same lens may view different aspects of the ethical picture. This strengthens the argument for board diversity in gender, age, experience, knowledge and culture.

We would like to take a moment to explain the rationale and epistemology behind the kaleidoscope we developed. Epistemology is the theory of knowledge, dealing with the question 'How do we know what we know?'.[5] One of the core epistemologies assumes that organisations (including their management and governance structures) are social constructions, built on communication and processes of meanings. Constructionism argues that truth is neither absolute nor objective, but is constructed by people's minds. Constructing or making knowledge is not a passive, but an active process.[6] Meanings are discovered through a process that involves the individual's interpretation.[7] This process is strongly influenced by our sociocultural background; we construct our interpretations based on our background, which includes our values, beliefs, practices[8] and traditions that 'shape what we are and how we understand the world'.[9]

A great example of constructing knowledge happened a few years ago, when Zivit joined an organisation and, during her the first week, the global CEO came for a visit in Australia. In his meeting for all staff in a Melbourne townhouse, the CEO said: 'Read my lips, there will not be any redundancies in Australia in the next year'. As soon as the meeting concluded, people started preparing their résumés (including the new employees) and the office was buzzing with speculations as to when the redundancies would start and which departments will be included this time. People explained to Zivit that, previously, when the CEO said that there would not be any redundancies, as soon as he left Australia there was a major redundancy wave. They interpreted his words by constructing the knowledge based on their past experience with him and the new employees based their knowledge on their colleagues' experience. They were correct – two weeks after he left, the redundancies commenced. The point is that, in their next organisation, once they hear a similar message, they will interpret it based on their experience with the previous employer.

Another aspect of the constructivist epistemology that is highly relevant for the kaleidoscope is that the 'truth' is a sociocultural concept. Each society has its own perception of the truth, including: what can be accepted as truth, which values reflect the acquisition of truth and what is the status of people who tell the truth. This makes the governance of ethics in the global environment a very complex task. On the one hand, board members govern based on an analysis of the reality or the 'truth' that is influenced by their own sociocultural background. On the other hand, they need to make decisions in countries and cultures that are foreign to their own cultural and ethical systems.

To make things even more challenging, knowledge is socially constructed. People create meanings through social processes such as communications and interactions.[10] The boardroom is a great place to demonstrate this process. The dynamic between the board members themselves and the board and executives shapes the discussions and decisions – not to mention the dependency of boards on information provided by the executives. We strongly recommend that board members keep this in mind when preparing for board meetings, during the meetings and when reflecting on the meetings afterwards. Having a diverse board and bearing in mind the construction of knowledge helps in governing the ethical system and directing the company to a successful future.

Notes

1 See https://www.themonthly.com.au/issue/2015/august/1438351200/catherine-ford/department-disgrace [26 July 2016].
2 Available at http://www.behindthebarcode.org.au/ [26 July 2016].
3 See https://en.wikipedia.org/wiki/2013_Savar_building_collapse [26 July 2016].
4 See http://www.dailymail.co.uk/news/article-2103798/Revealed-Inside-Apples-Chinese-sweatshop-factory-workers-paid-just-1-12-hour.html [26 July 2016].
5 Crotty, M. (1998) *The Foundation of Social Research: Meaning and Perspective in the Research Process*, London, Sage Publications, p. 8.
6 Denzin, N. K. and Lincoln, Y. S. (2000) *The Sage Handbook of Qualitative Research* (2nd edn), London, Sage.
7 Grondin, J. (1994) *Introduction to Philosophical Hermeneutics*, J. Weinsheimer (transl.), New Haven, CT, Yale University Press.
8 Denzin and Lincoln (2000) op. cit.
9 Gallagher, S. (1992). *Hermeneutics and Education*, Albany, State University of New York Press, p. 87.
10 Gergen, K. J. (1985) The social constructionist movement in modern psychology, *American Psychologist*, Vol. 40, No. 3, pp. 266–275.

7   What about the future?

Thoughts and recommendations for boards

It is a truism to state that the pace of change has accelerated over recent years and it is highly unlikely that it will slow down. It is also clear that, as we have illustrated, the issue of ethics in corporate governance is also receiving increasing attention. This creates new opportunities for directors that include:

- the need to take an increasingly dynamic approach to risk;
- the need for increasing attention to cyber security;
- the need to develop new skills through education and retraining in order to cope with change;
- the need to handle escalating challenges relating to the economics and scale of infrastructure;
- international trade and political volatility with shifting alliances and trading opportunities;
- health and safety issues that concern not only today but carry potential liability for negative effects over the very long term;
- dealing with disruptive technologies and approaches.

All of these aspects are going to create new challenges from an ethical perspective. It is a relatively easy matter to deal with these when yours is the only organisation facing them but the situation changes quickly when competitors enter the same space. Under these conditions the importance of having very clear and precisely specified behavioural values capable of guiding people in terms of what is and what is not ethical activity becomes apparent. Coupled with this is the importance of behaviour modelling by all those with leadership responsibility – from the chairman of directors right down to those in the most junior supervisory positions. It only needs a small number of people to act in inappropriate ways for cognitive dissonance to develop and, under such circumstances, people will always see the truth as being what they observe rather than what they hear.

If inappropriate (i.e. unethical) behaviour is not confronted or, even worse, is actually rewarded in any way, then even the most ethical culture can quickly be seduced into an 'end justifies the means' approach.

As Sir John Harvey-Johns pointed out,[1] while the board has a collective responsibility in relation to this, ultimately it is the chairman who must be held accountable for all organisational performance issues – including ethics – because it is with the chairman that finally 'the buck stops'.

Recommendations for boards

We decided to end the book with a list of recommendations provided by interviewees as to how to direct and govern ethical organisations. The recommendations are organised according to the kaleidoscope lenses but our initial recommendations are given below:

1   The kaleidoscope is only as good as the person who looks through it. A diverse group looking through each of the lenses will have a wider view than a group of directors from the same background, gender, age and culture.
2   We recommend that ethics in general becomes a common agenda item in each board meeting as part of the meeting evaluation.
3   Each of the lenses should be reconsidered carefully, on at least a yearly basis, at a specially convened 'ethics and the board' meeting.

Lens 1: External risks

- Assess where the company is located on both financial goals and societal mores or impacts. Is this the ethical stand that you would like to take and where you think the company should be in the long term? If not, where would the board like to position the company strategically?
- Develop a long-term ethical statement that will become a tool for gaining strategic advantage. Reinvent the relationship between the business and society to ensure long-term sustainability.
- Board agenda should include open discussions about:
  - external and internal conflicts and paradoxes;
  - ethical dilemmas that affect the long term (future generations, environment, society at large), not only short-term or immediate risk;
  - proactive risk management – not the response to risk, but the way the company should manage risk.

- Ensure that the risk policy:

    o addresses ethics and ethical decision making;
    o clarifies the board's risk appetite.

- Questions for board members to ask themselves:

    o Am I prepared for this to be on the front page of the newspaper?
    o Will I be proud to tell my family and friends about this decision?
    o Will I feel or experience any possible personal embarrassment if I have to defend this action?

- The risk committee should have ethics on its agenda at every meeting.

Market transparency

- Are we keeping the market and investors informed? Develop a strategy/statement which defines guidelines to striking a balance between informing the market (legal and ethical obligations) and keeping confidentiality that is needed for a strategic advantage.

Investors and lobbying groups

Boards should discuss the relevant groups and their agendas and define a strategic approach to ensure proactive ethical management of communications with these groups.

Lens 2: Internal processes

Management

- Even when the organisation is very successful (and perhaps *especially* when the company is very successful), boards need to remember their governance role and, despite great relationships with the CEO and executives, continue probing the information received from the executive team:

    o Does the information really represent the sample? Do we receive the complete data? What information is missing? What do we need to know – the information that hasn't been brought to the board's attention? Is there anything else that we don't know about that is not presented by the management?
    o Management reports need to include complaints from shareholders, customers, employees, occupational health and safety reports, updates to market and shareholders, social media comment. Ask the executives about the rationale behind the

information that is reported and what is not being analysed and incorporated into the reports.

o   Even when you trust the management team, remember that they tend to tell you what they think you want to hear. This is natural. Always probe and seek to receive different perspectives.

- Review the compensation package offered to the CEO and the executive team. Is this in line with the ethical standards that the board sets for the organisation? The board should discuss questions, such as:

o   The total package that the CEO receives – what ethical message does it send to employees and stakeholders?

o   Bonuses – do they encourage achievement of short- or long-term goals?

o   Salary increases – we have seen some companies increasing salaries to the top management in years when employees had no increases. These boards should have discussed the ethical message that this practice sends.

o   What is it that the CEO and executives are remunerated for? Ensure that long-terms goals are part of the key performance indicators (KPIs) and that bonuses are awarded for achievement of long-term goals. Ensure that no drastic moves have been made in order to achieve individual KPIs for remuneration purposes; for example, CEOs who make major redundancies to reduce costs and achieve their bonus. Is it right to pay bonuses and salary increases to executives, while the rest of the organisation is subject to a salary freeze? What is the ethical message that such a board decision sends to employees and stakeholders?

Marketing

- The board needs to define the ethical guidelines to marketing – including what is said in any advertising.
- Incorporate ethics as part of the company brand.
- Directors must be in touch with customers and hear about their experience of the organisation to ensure that marketing sets the right expectations.

Complaints management

- The board should review reports about complaints of customers, employees, stakeholders, partners and suppliers on a regular basis. These reports should encourage a productive discussion about the following points:

o How is the organisation perceived?
o What are the pain points?
o What stands behind the net promoter score (NPS) of our customers and our employees? Is there a connection between both results?

Supply chain

- Boards need to decide on the supply chain code of conduct and ethical demands and communicate these widely. This must include all stages of the supply chain from raw materials to finished product or service.
- Boards then need to ensure that the policy is implemented and that audits are carried out on a regular basis, including:

o quality control;
o contract management;
o compliance monitoring;
o supplier hiring processes and removal of non-compliant suppliers;
o ethical treatment of workers (regardless of their employment status, such as full time, part time, casual or contract) at all levels and at all times.

Procurement

- Boards need to ensure that the procurement policy and guidelines are in place and enforced, including:

o identification and management of conflicts of interests;
o proper use of the position (and specific guidelines on acceptance of gifts and hospitality);
o guidelines for ethical dealings with potential suppliers and tenderers;
o guidelines for use of public resources.

Lens 3: Board risks

Conflict of interest

- The chairperson must at all times check the ethical conduct and performance of the non-executive and executive board members. The chair needs to actively and mindfully look for behaviours that indicate self-interest among directors before checking the company for illegal and unethical behaviours.

- Board members should be involved in what is happening in the organisation beyond participating in a monthly meeting. Their movement around the company should ensure that they are informed about what is going on, rather than seeking to govern by making assumptions about the management of the organisation. Remember that it takes time for ethical issues to escalate into a crisis and that even when organisations achieve their goals, unethical practices might be used. In the long term, ignoring these practices is a recipe for failure.
- Ethics should be one of the areas addressed at the board performance reviews (as well as in the performance reviews of executives and all other employees).
- Have a clear process for addressing illegal and unethical behaviours at board level, including investigation processes and criteria for dismissing directors for ethical as well as legal reasons.
- Have clear and enforced rules in place for conflicts of interest. Board members with conflicts should not be around the table during the discussions, not just excluded during the voting. They should not be allowed to voice their opinion about the issues at any stage leading up to, or at the time of, any decision being made.
- There is an element of ethics in every decision the board makes. Hence, we believe that the board needs to incorporate a question about ethics as part of the decision-making process. Even if a decision is legal, we still need to ask 'Is it right?'.
- Conduct yearly board ethics training – including ethics in general and the specific ethical issues that the organisation is facing.
- Include ethics as part of the board nomination and recruitment process. Do not nominate new directors without having a clear understanding of their ethical values and ensuring that they align with those of the board. Check that their stated values are also those demonstrated in their behaviour.

Lens 4: Organisational culture

Understanding the organisational culture at all its levels and in all its complexity is a task that many boards perceive as difficult to measure. However, there are many ways to know and assess what is really going on in the organisation. They all start with moving away from the procedural or detached board culture.

- Walk the floor and ask for people's informal opinions about the organisation, its culture and ethics. Use your intuition to determine if there is a need for empirical data.

- Meet with the CEO and executive team regularly, with no agenda. The main purpose of this is just to talk about what keeps them awake at night.
- Lead by example – do the right thing.
- The board's culture sets the tone for the organisation:
  - Create a culture that allows executives to confidently bring issues to the board's attention without being afraid that this will bite them back.
  - A couple of chairpersons suggested leaving the boardroom doors open, so people can hear their discussions. This will send a message that the board is transparent; hence, the entire organisation should be as well.
  - Create a board culture that is open, not arrogant and encourages people to raise issues.
  - Have open discussions about the values that guide board decisions. How does the board convey these values to the executive team? Are these values communicated to the management team by the executive team?
  - As a board member you have to be questioning, but be careful of the 'how'. No bullying in the boardroom please!

- Set clear ethical expectations and review the ethics programme regularly:
  - Design the ethical system (clearly stating what ethics means to the company) with clear behavioural standards. Needless to say, model these behaviours.
  - Ensure that people have confidence in the whistleblowing procedures.
  - What licence does the board give to the CEO in terms of behaviour?
  - Does the organisation have an effective ethics programme? Engage external surveys to determine how many employees observed misconduct versus how many of them reported it? Do employees feel under pressure to compromise on standards? What are the consequences of reporting misconduct (is there ever any retaliation)?

- Measure the organisational culture:
  - Conduct regular internal cultural audits using external consultants.
  - Look at voluntary turnover across the organisation and the reasons for it. Also, be aware of areas in which there is frequent and/or regular involuntary turnover.

- Look at the leave balances. Consider the utilisation of personal (sick) leave and compare it to the national average. When higher than the benchmark, it can be a sign of management and ethical issues (such as bullying, stress, etc.). High annual leave balances could potentially show the following:

  - employees are not allowed or are afraid to take leave (indicating a management problem that could be connected to planning, productivity and ethics);
  - employees are not reporting their leave – meaning that the management is turning a blind eye to employees failing to follow the rules;
  - employees are afraid that, in their absence, some form of illegal or otherwise inappropriate behaviour might be inadvertently uncovered.

- Conduct employee opinion surveys to measure the following:

  - Whether the leaders (according to the different levels) are perceived as fair and trustworthy.
  - What are the true company values that guide decision making at all the organisational levels? Are they similar to the stated values?
  - Review the whistleblowing policy and its implementation. What are the consequences or ramifications of exposing unethical behaviours in the organisation? This could be asked in a periodically conducted anonymous ethics survey for the team or a random sample of the team (in large organisations).
  - Ask executives how their decisions benefit other business areas within the organisation.
  - Enquire whether celebration of success takes place at the lower levels of the organisation, not only acknowledging the top levels.

- Such surveys should be conducted by an independent third party organisation that, apart from a contract to conduct the survey, has no other direct or indirect link to the organisation or to any person employed by or associated in any other way with the organisation.

- Empower the HR department to lead ethics training:

  - Conduct ethics training at every organisational level. At the end of the training, HR must ask for formal feedback from participants about areas that cause concern. Areas of concern should be reported to the board and lessons from the feedback need to be embedded in current and new policies and processes.

- Diversity – to truly prosper in the global arena, the following diversities are important:

  o Board diversity – culture, gender, age, experience (expertise) and education.
  o Management diversity – does the top management represent the cultural diversity both of where the organisation operates and of its customer base?

Lens 5: Intuition

- Look for patterns in language that reveal a lack of personal accountability, for example 'We had no control' (or, as in one company in which Doug was consulting, when an employee tells the board that 'profit here is a random end variable').
- Look for signs that the management team is trying to control the board; examples include the following:

  o Providing too much detail so that the board can't cope adequately with the information.
  o Providing too little detail or details that point in the wrong direction.
  o Covering up bad news or not reporting bad news in a timely fashion or reporting the news only after finding a 'solution'.
  o Ask management about the information they are relying on to make a given recommendation. If the information differs from what was presented to the board, ask to see it and for an explanation of any discrepancies.
  o When the management team is perceived as always telling the truth yet seldom or never tells 'the whole truth' except under serious questioning.

- Look at body language and responses to questions by board members and executives.

Note

1 Sir John Harvey-Johns, *The Company Chairman* (2012) (as quoted in Long, D. G. (2012) *Third Generation Leadership and the Locus of Control: Knowledge, Change and Neuroscience*, Gower Publishing, UK).

Epilogue

We would like to end the book by re-emphasising the difference between acting legally and acting ethically. In focusing solely on the letter of the law, companies ignore the important question – 'Is this the right thing to do?' Overlooking this ethical question poses a major risk for an organisation's long-term sustainability. Hence, this question should be an integral part of the organisational culture. A company's organisational culture is not based on policies and posters of values on the wall, it is the actual behaviours of and decisions made by the leadership, starting at the board level. As can be seen from the case of VW and other examples in the book, boards that rely too heavily on policies and reports put their companies at ethical risk, opening the door for unethical decisions to be made at various organisational levels.

Another aspect of the organisational culture is diversity. True diversity (in terms of gender, age, culture, education, experience, etc.) is key to looking at issues from different perspectives, understanding ethical dilemmas, making the right decision and gaining strategic advantage. Having people who come from the same background and share the same experiences (especially when they have worked together for many years) looking through the different lenses of the ethics kaleidoscope can still result in group thinking. Diversity of thought at the boardroom level will ensure better decision making and use of the kaleidoscope.

Finally, we hope that after reading this book you will mindfully consider ethics, both in each board meeting and in the board's yearly plan. We would like to encourage boards to consider the question of ethics as part of their regular decision-making processes. On a yearly basis, when reviewing strategy, marketing, governance and other business aspects, we encourage boards to examine them via the ethical lens. This will ensure that the board is not only responding to crisis, but is proactively managing and gaining a sustainable strategic advantage from the application of ethics.

We argue in this book that, in addition to strategy, governance and hiring/firing the CEO, the board also plays an important and active role in leading the corporate ethics for sustainable success.

Index